MW01615595

HAWAI`I WAYS

Living in Two Worlds

Rochelle delaCruz

Hanakahi Press
2016

ISBN: 0692802401
ISBN 13 9780692802403

Cover Photo by Man Chong Wong
Mu`umu`u by Ida Mae Wong

Hanakahi Press
P.O. Box 782
Hilo, Hawai`i 96720
www.hanakahipress.com

For my children and grandchildren who can always come home to Hawai`i.

TABLE OF CONTENTS

INTRODUCTION

These stories come from my own place of puzzlement. While managing my two worlds of Hilo, Hawai`i where I grew up and Seattle, Washington where I worked, I often found myself stumbling over gestures, behaviors, words and ideas. Bemused, I started writing about these predicaments in order to make sense of them. What you will be reading are intersections where my two worlds not only crossed but sometimes collided. Luckily, laughter lit my way through the mazes and minefields and to help you come along with me, I have provided a glossary of local words.

First, let me say something about my primary point of reference Hawai`i, an isolated archipelago of islands in the middle of the Pacific Ocean. But who doesn't know about this wondrous place? What many may not be aware of however, are the two populations overlapping in these beautiful isles that make Hawai`i what it is today.

The first are the Native Hawaiians who created a culture rich in stories and traditions. Theirs is the world view that still dominates Hawai`i even after centuries of bias and suppression by foreign influences. And since the 1970s, the Hawaiians have been reviving their language and relearning ancient skills such as sailing thousands of miles across the ocean in double-hulled canoes using for guidance only the stars and signs of nature. They are recovering neglected and overrun lo`i to grow kalo to be made into poi, the delicious staple from old days. Many are returning to other traditional Hawaiian practices, doing as their ancestors did generations ago.

So who's Hawaiian?

In most states, it is fairly easy to claim native status by virtue of birth but being born in Hawai`i does not make you Hawaiian. As with Native Alaskan and Native American, to be Native Hawaiian requires *genealogy* – Hawaiian bloodline. Sometimes you are asked to provide this genealogy by tracing family lineage as far back as possible. While all of us with generations of history in these islands are deeply influenced by Hawaiian people and ways, we do not call ourselves Hawaiian unless we have genealogy.

The secondary island culture includes other ethnicities, mostly from Asia and around the Pacific who have settled here since 1778, the year Captain James Cook charted the main islands on the map for the Western World. This group is referred to as "local", comprising not only traditions and descendants of settlers who were recruited by haole to work on the sugar plantations beginning in 1835 but also the Hawaiians whose culture informs everything and everyone in Hawai`i.

Hawaiian was the dominant language until the illegal 1898 American takeover of Hawai`i following the overthrow of Queen Lili`uokalani. Soon after, English became the requirement in public schools and government. This prohibition of native language gave rise to what is known in linguistic circles as Hawaii Creole English but what we locals refer to simply as "Pidgin."

Pidgin arose out of the need to communicate among the diverse groups brought in to work on the plantations. Foreign laborers mixed words and phrases from their native tongue with Hawaiian, the language of the land and English, the language of plantation owners and managers. After the 1898 takeover, Pidgin became the common idiom of many island inhabitants including Hawaiians whose language went underground.

Today, Pidgin is an identity marker for islanders. When we hear it, we know the speaker is from Hawai`i. But tread carefully if you are not a native Pidgin speaker. Even though linguists have outlined its grammar, syntax, vocabulary, pronunciation and intonation, it is a language not easily learned. Because of its sociopolitical origins, local ears can quickly discern non-natives who might sound as if they are mocking islanders when they attempt to speak it.

My stories come from the local experience, thanks to a family line that goes back to ancestors' 1880s arrival in these islands to work the sugar plantations on the Hāmākua coast of Hawai`i Island. They reflect a way of life that evolved from plantation days when laborers immigrated from China, Japan, Portugal, Korea, the Philippines and other places. What you will read in *Hawai`i Ways* comes from a clash between what I learned while growing up in Hawai`i before statehood in 1959 and American ways and attitudes I've encountered either here in the Islands or on the continent.

Perhaps reading about my befuddling intersections will help you ponder some of yours. As you reflect on the various ways to negotiate the world around us, you might begin to see these Hawaiian Islands and its people in a different light.

ACKNOWLEDGEMENTS

I was born in Hilo, Hawai`i, grew up in a large, extended family and graduated from Hilo High School in 1963, four years after Hawai`i became the 50th state in the U.S. Upon graduation, I left my beloved islands for the first time to travel to a foreign land, the University of Washington. My adventures began as soon as I got off the plane in Seattle and encountered others who looked, walked and talked different, smelled, dressed and ate different. Quickly I learned to find my way around a campus larger than my hometown only to end up disoriented in vast lecture halls. I lived in a dormitory with young women interested in "Hawaya" who winced when they tasted li hing mui from my stash of crack seed but in return, made me gag when they ate rice with milk and sugar. They laughed when Hawai`i students ran outside into the first snow of the year in our slippers and we howled when they asked what it was like to live in grass houses.

After graduating from UW, I got married, had three children and received an MA from the University of Hawai`i at Mānoa before settling back in Washington State where I taught English-as-a-Second Language for twenty-eight years at Seattle Central Community College. When students in my classes asked for some explanation on certain kinds of "American behavior," I realized that even though I came from the 50th State, I had much in common with these foreign students. Despite all the time and energy trying to adapt to living on the continent, I too was still busily working through my own dilemmas.

Over the course of thirty years in the Pacific Northwest, I came home to Hilo to visit family and friends as often as time and money permitted. Going back and forth, I frequently found myself perplexed by that strange world beyond the reef. With countless Pacific crossings, I began to notice that in Hilo the world looks like this but in Seattle it looks like that. I started writing about these divergent views and recorded them for public and community radio stations in Hawai`i and Washington where they aired for over ten years. Those stories are the basis for the ones presented here but expanded and revised for reading rather than listening.

In addition to teaching and radio work, I was editor and publisher of a free community newspaper in Seattle, *Northwest Hawai`i Times*, a gathering place for Hawai`i people far from home. For five years (2004 to 2009) we collected articles, stories, photos, events, recipes and anything else islanders wanted to contribute, then laid them out in newspaper format that went to press every month. All volunteers, we distributed da pepa in an elaborate system of tag, with Hawai`i-connected people around Puget Sound ready and waiting to receive bundles to deliver to locations in their areas. It was a true community effort where anyone interested could participate in whatever way they chose: writing, photographing, advertising, distributing etc. I will always keep close to my heart the many transplanted islanders in the Pacific Northwest who were an integral part of *Northwest Hawai`i Times*. Mahalo to all who helped with this good fun, worthwhile endeavor and the best collaborative project I have ever worked on. The print version of the newspaper ceased in 2009 but digital archives can still be accessed at northwesthawaiitimes.com.

I would like to thank public radio stations in Hawai`i and Washington State for airing my stories. Special mahalo and aloha to KBCS in Bellevue, Washington which not only continues to promote and support Hawaiian music programs for homesick islanders but also put my stories up in a podcast. I am equally indebted to the many inquisitive students from other countries who asked pertinent questions that forced me to explore our behavior patterns and am deeply grateful to friends and radio listeners who kept urging me to publish these cross-cultural insights.

I especially want to thank my family for the loving encouragement they have always given me, along with the nuggets of family history that occasionally turn up in these stories. Aloha nui goes to my biggest fan and supporter Roy, who has cheered me on through the years and made all of this possible.

I hope you enjoy reading these stories as much as I have enjoyed writing them.

Me ke aloha pumehana,
Rochelle
October 2016
Hilo, Hawai`i

CHAPTER 1

CONNECTIONS

Whenever I introduce myself in Seattle, I say something like "Hi. Rochelle delaCruz." I know that my new acquaintance will take this cue to volunteer her name, Jane Smith for example. And now that the introductions are over, Rochelle delaCruz and Jane Smith have properly met and will proceed to a riveting exchange about the weather.

But in Hawai`i, one of the first questions after (or even before) the exchange of names is *Where you wen grad?* Translation: Where did you graduate from high school? The answer is fraught with information. But even after I introduce myself as Rochelle delaCruz, Hilo High, people still have their eyebrows up expectantly and I know I'm not yet done.

They're waiting for the connections. So after I say my name, I add this tidbit. "My father is Wong. Post Office Wong" since everyone of a certain age knows my father who worked the main window at Hilo Post Office for thirty years. If by some slim chance they don't know him, then I move on to the Shoe Shop Lady because my mother used to be at one of the downtown stores and over a period of twenty-five years, put shoes on all of the feet in Hilo, Puna and the Hāmākua Coast.

If, by some fluke the person I'm meeting knows neither my father nor my mother, they'll know my brother, the school teacher who is also a musician and has played at most of the wedding, funeral, anniversary and birthday parties around the island.

Once however, none on my list of illustrious family members was known to my new friend who I figured must have just arrived from the planet Pluto.

Momentarily stumped I had one more ace in my pocket, my other brother who has been living in Honolulu since he graduated from Hilo High School many years ago but rarely do I have to pull him out. This time I did and guess what. Pluto knew him.

Conversations in Hilo often sound like this. "You remember Beatrice! Her mother-in-law used to work 'Ono Pastry before she went Kresses fountain! Her brother is married to Geraldine's first husband's sistah!"

Let me warn you right now that should you find yourself in the middle of one of these conversations, pay close attention or else you'll get lost amid all the connections.

And what everybody will suspect, is that you are not from Hilo.

CHAPTER 2

MAPS

I'm a great map reader when I'm in Seattle. I'm able to show you the four compass points and explain useful information such as: *streets* run east-west; *avenues* go north-south; *house numbers* indicate cross streets; stuff like that. I can direct you to the college where I teach by saying, "From the Ballard Bridge, go south on Elliott then east on Denny. You'll see the Space Needle to the north. After a couple of miles, take a right on Broadway – you'll be heading south again and the college is the red brick building at the corner of Pine."

But don't ask me for directions when I'm in Hilo. Not unless you are prepared to deal with "Just go down Waiānuenue till you come to the bay. Turn right and head Puna. If you go over the airplane bridge – some call it the singing bridge - you'll be going Hāmākua – wrong way! The bridge you want is Wailoa. Go straight over and hang another right by the Pancake House. You'll be heading Volocano."

A visitor to Hilo was looking for a church in Keaukaha one Sunday morning and ran into me. "Oh, OK," I said. "Just go down Waiānuenue till you come to the bay..." I told him exactly how to get to the church, but I could see he was glazing over.

3

"Will I be heading north?" he inquired.

"I have no idea but first, you have to go makai." I said, pointing down to the ocean.

He thanked me then jumped in his car and drove mauka auwē.

In Hawai`i, I have no notion of compass direction. I only know the southernmost tip of the Big Island Ka Lae, is also called South Point but I have no idea when I'm facing it unless I can see the sun. I know that Hilo is on the east side of the island because I'm able to watch the sunrise if it isn't raining. And Kona is on the west side because of its spectacular sunsets. But other than this knowledge which depends on the sun, I have no idea when I'm heading north, south, east or west when I am on Hawai`i Island.

The city of Honolulu on O`ahu is confusing to me. I'm usually there just to change planes on my way in or out of Hilo but when I do stay over, I have to remind myself that I am still in the Islands. With high rise buildings, multi-lane highways and bumper-to-bumper traffic, it could be California but it is freeway signage that throws me off the most. As I'm driving the Pali Highway from Kailua to go visit my auntie in Pālolo, a sign announces the up-coming ramp: *H1-East.* EAST?! Which way is East? Mulling this over I always miss the exit because it looks like it will take me in the opposite direction to `Aiea. So then I have to make some fast turnarounds to get back on track to Kaimukī so I can turn into Pālolo Valley.

When I am in Seattle on the edge of a vast continent, I have to know compass direction so that if I'm heading south to Oregon, I don't end up going east toward Montana with the possibility of ending up in Minnesota. But I don't need to know this in Hawai`i where our patterns are circular and I wish that freeway sign in Honolulu could be changed from *H1-East* to *H1-Diamond Head.*

This I could handle and it's not because I can't read maps.

CHAPTER 3

GARDEN

After we moved into our house in Seattle, I spent the first year staring at a tiny plot of ground that used to be a garden when it had different owners. There was even a small, open brick structure which I studied and finally concluded that in spite of its odd shape, it must be a barbecue pit. I was later informed by a friendly neighbor that it was the place for a compost pile. Oooooh I nodded, without a clue what compost was, let alone a compost pile. Later when I found out, I was still puzzled. OK so there's composting, alkaline soil, southern exposure…but what did this have to do with me and my garden?

I come from Hilo, Hawai`i where we have to be careful what we throw off our porch because it'll grow…up the stairs and into the house if you let it. But things are different in Seattle where gardening requires not only physical work but mental labor as well. Sometimes I have to read a book and then think about what to do.

So I thought about what I liked, planned out my garden and started with Chinese long beans. But all I got were a few stunted pods hanging on for dear life to sickly vines. I then chose what I assumed were easier crops but when the fail-safe tomato failed, I gave up on vegetables and moved on to flowers.

But even the flowers defied me. I tried everything: sweet peas soaked twenty-four hours before planting on Presidents' Day; store-bought color-coordinated starter petunias and lobelia; nursery-guaranteed rose bushes. I scattered two packages of wild flower seeds in that back patch one spring but all that came up were a few pitiful poppies. I learned the hard way about *bulbs* – those infernal daffodils and tulips – which I planted, wrong way down the first time. A few managed to turn themselves upright and even sprouted, surely a sign of plant intelligence but also a hint that some bulbs are smarter than some gardeners.

I can't tell you how happy I am every time I return to Hilo where I take the green top from the white pineapple or the white bottom from the green onion and poke them in the dirt, knowing they won't let me down. Or I find a forgotten orchid quietly blooming in a broken clay pot filled with lava rocks. Or I stick poles into the ground as fast as possible to outrun the ever-sprouting bittermelon that will climb them.

Finally this year, I left Hilo with a new plan for my garden in Seattle. In over twenty-five years in the Pacific Northwest I've tried almost everything but it's time to stop fooling around. This new garden I'm planning won't depend on the seasons or the climate nor tempt the slugs or the aphids. It won't ever be in need of compost or mulch or fertilizer and there'll be no testing of soil. Instead, my new garden will aim for a higher aesthetic, its beauty enhanced by moss and its harvest, a feast for the eyes.

A rock garden. That's what I'm planning in Seattle. After all these years of fighting with nature, I'm going to just go with her instead.

Brilliant, don't you think?

CHAPTER 4

FREEZER

Yesterday as I was opening the freezer in my mother's house in Hilo, I was warned to not let anything fall on my foot because it could get broken – my foot as well as the frozen laulau. When I finally gently popped the door and saw that the freezer was jammed packed, quick I slammed it back shut again. But what's the point of a freezer if you're afraid to see what's in there for fear of breaking a toe? So then I challenged my mother to go two weeks without buying food.

"Let's eat what we already have in the freezer," I said to her. It seemed to be a reasonable idea but when she answered with stink eye, I suspected it was a touchy subject. This was confirmed when my father jumped up practically shouting, "That's what I tell her but never mind if get ten pounds pork butt already in the freezer. If on sale, gotta buy!"

Not only that but when there's a limit on the number of things we can buy on special, she rises to the challenge by taking all of us along. "OK, you buy two cans tuna, you buy two and you buy two. Here's the money...No, *take* it. Me, I'm going buy my two cans, take them to the car then go back in for two more."

Her tactics are relentless. Supermarkets in Hilo don't stand a chance.

My mother can't resist buying on sale even though she has multiples of everything. She admits that maybe she has to be careful with what's in the freezer but the paper, canned and bottled goods will keep for a long time. I open the cupboard to find half a dozen gallons of oil, too tall to stand upright, lying side by side like good children down for their afternoon nap. I'm thinking: there's enough oil in this house alone to sponsor the next bodybuilders' competition.

Don't tell Mom that sometimes in Seattle, I run out of staples. She would be disappointed that I didn't learn better because when we're shopping, I often hear her say, "No need now but better pick up on sale before we run out." What's worse, when I get caught short and she's not around, I might send one of the kids to the store. Kids! Who are attracted to shiny objects and have built-in radar directing them to the most expensive brand. They're especially talented at picking up some product that I'll never use unless I completely run out of food during a snowstorm, which would be the equivalent of hell freezing over because of the way their grandmother stocks our cupboard every time she visits Seattle.

My mother tries to understand my lack of interest in accumulating food and paper products while I grapple with her vocation in gathering and storing. I think it's evolved over a lifetime of living on an island, making sure that the next shipping strike doesn't catch them without rice or chicken broth. After all, Mom was a big hero when she went to Oʻahu during the last strike. In addition to her usual omiyage box of Hilo fishcake, she also packed a suitcase full with rolls of toilet paper, bought on sale and stored in the back of closets and under the beds in her house in Hilo.

Friends and family in Honolulu cheered.

CHAPTER 5

FAT

I was fat when I was a child in Hilo and whenever I went to church on Sunday in my best clothes, the strap from the black patent-leather Mary Jane shoes made a perfect mound of stockinged flesh at the top of my foot. I liked to buckle it tight that way because the bulge reminded me of a loaf of Portuguese sweet bread, our standard Sunday-after-church breakfast. But then my brother looked down and frowned. He whispered, "Look your feet. You too fat. You going Hell if you no lose weight."

"Hah? What?" I softly protested. "But, but Hell is…for killing and stealing. Not for fat! Fat is maybe Purgatory, but not Hell!"

There was a postcard in our family album of the Fat Lady, a nameless beauty who sold pictures of her chubby self when she came through Hilo with the traveling circus long ago. No one ever admitted to buying this photo but there she was among our family treasures. Once, my brother propped her image in the refrigerator against the jar of guava jelly then hid until I strolled through the kitchen in my frequent and endless quest for snacks. When I opened the refrigerator door and screamed to see the half-naked Fat Lady smiling at me, he leapt out of the broom closet.

"That's going be you if you no stop eating. Bettah watch out cuz the boys not going dance with you. And anyway it's a sin to be fat. Because eating too much is a sin. So you bettah stop eating," was his brotherly advice. I glared at him, grabbed the jelly, threw open the cover, scooped some out with my fingers and stuck it in my mouth.

This shows you how conflicted and confused we were and still are about fat and skinny.

As proof of our confusion, pick up any women's magazine and look at the cover: "yum" strawberry-banana split or "incredible" key lime pie or the "ultimate" German chocolate cake, all of which make my eyes glaze, my mouth gape and drool dribble down my chin.

But wait. As I tear my eyes away from the magazine cover with the chocolate heart-shaped vanilla ice cream sandwich, confectioner's sugar powdering over a star cut-out decorated on a plate with candied cherries and kalakoa sprinkles around a mocha truffle swimming in raspberry sauce, I read small words screaming in red:

"Lose Pounds Fast!"
"Cholesterol: Should you worry?"
"25 Everyday Fat Fighters!"
"I lost 165 lbs!"
"The Miracle Diet!"
"109 ways to look thinner!"
"7 Diet Traps – What's ruining yours?"

Maybe these kinds of magazines, I'm thinking.

Are you caught in the middle of mixed messages about fat and skinny the way I am? What other country on earth has liposuction, eating disorders, gym and fitness industries alongside fat-food franchises, doughnut chains and warehouses that sell in such bulk that one muffin could feed a family of four? Where else do people order a scoop of vanilla ice cream over Dutch apple pie with hot cinnamon sauce and then put a packet of sugar substitute in the accompanying cup of coffee? It makes me crazy. It drives me nuts!

You know what? Just give me another piece of that pie...yes ala mode... with sauce ganfannit.

CHAPTER 6

PETS

There a big difference between pets in Seattle and pets in Hilo. Dogs in Seattle often sport Irish-knit sweaters and bandanas, cats wear jeweled collars and both have scheduled appointments for regular checkups, nail clips, teeth cleaning and flea baths. They sleep in wicker beds with designer covers and eat gourmet pet food in personalized china. Cats lounge at a cat café in downtown Seattle where patrons pay for the privilege of petting them while dogs get pampered at a place offering herbal spas and formal grooming, in preparation for the prom I presume. In between meals, cats nibble on store-bought snacks that claim to taste "better than mice!" and dogs get treated to "pup-eroni." Some of them are even hauled around in a stroller or a baby back pack and taught to dance the foxtrot.

This is too much work if you ask me.

When I was growing up in Hilo, dogs I knew were considered lucky if they got a real bone to gnaw on after the family dinner and snacked on whatever the nearest human was munching: kakimochi, sour lemon, malassadas. They stayed outdoors, roamed the countryside and napped in the middle of the street. They rarely wore a collar and never a bandana...too hot in Hawai`i and the other dogs might laugh.

Back then, dogs and cats had names that told us they were canines and felines but nowadays in the Northwest, I have to wonder whatever happened to Spot, Kitty, Fido, Rover as I get introduced to pets named Lisa, Charlie, Ellen and Jimmy. On the continent, I always have to pay close attention when someone is fretting over Minerva's eye infection to figure out if they're talking about their sister, daughter, mother-in-law or Chihuahua.

In Seattle I have a cat, Henry, named by his former owner. I would have called him Whiskers or Claws. Henry gets mail – a postcard reminding him to come in for his annual check up and shots. One time, the vet diagnosed him as dehydrated and suffering from stress but how can a cat suffer from stress? Trying to decide which sunny spot to sleep in today? On which upholstered chair to spread dander? Which bird to safely clack at behind double-paned windows?

"Perhaps we need to get to the source of his stress," intoned the vet. Thinking he was a nanosecond away from recommending a cat psychiatrist, I gave him `opelu eye, darting it between him and my worried children so he stopped talking. But the worst was when we were presented with the bill...52 bucks...for ten minutes and a shot. Hey! What about MY stress?

Pets I grew up with in Hilo used to run and hide when they heard their bath water filling up the galvanized washtub out in the yard twice a year. And the only vets we knew back then were old soldiers. But lately I've been alarmed by small signs of changing times. Recently I heard a veterinary radio ad about "the canine-human bond," advice on how your dog can get "a fair shake from the law," and what to do about "pudgy pets" with information on the "lower fat philosophy of feeding."

Watch out Hilo. Animal therapists in Seattle are probably at this moment coordinating their move to the new frontier, the Big Island. They'll come dedicated to the liberation of dogs and cats from owners who think of them as...dogs and cats.

Hold on.

CHAPTER 7

CAR BEHAVIOR

Does your behavior in a car depend on where you are, the way that mine does? I drive a car in Seattle, Washington and also in Hilo, Hawai`i but you wouldn't think it was the same person doing the driving.

In Hilo, I beep my horn – and only sometimes – when passing a friend. It's a short, cheerful toot-toot, not the long, leaned-into blast I use in Seattle when someone cuts in front of me or fails to notice the light change to green. On the island, I always let a car in ahead of me because I get rewarded with a smile and a wave from the driver. But in Seattle whenever I've let someone in, I've gotten not even a head bob so forget you Mister. I got places to go too.

Also in Hilo, the only gesturing I do from the car is a friendly hand wave and sometimes I get the shaka in return. I can't say that I actually use my hands for any kind of nonverbal signal in Seattle but it crosses my mind to do so, especially when I am the recipient of finger messages. So I'm often muttering to myself in the car in Seattle but never in Hilo. Too many people I know will see me and call to ask what's wrong.

On my morning commute in Seattle, I often notice – I'm sorry to say *women* drivers using their rear-view mirror to put on makeup at a stop light. I never see this in Hilo because women in my home town get dressed before leaving the house. We're quirky that way.

I had a student in Seattle who showed up to class one day with only one eye made up – eyeliner, eye shadow, mascara, the works. But the other eye was completely bare. You try managing a discussion of serious topics while facing a student with only one eye made up. As we talked about whether or not language directs one's view of the world, I wondered if that morning, the student stopped at only one light instead of her customary two. Does the morning traffic direct one's application of makeup? This never crosses my mind in Hilo.

I've been driving for decades and in Seattle, it shows. I follow the arterial, glide over floating bridges, turn on my lights when barreling through tunnels. I can safely cut across four lanes to exit the freeway or yield when entering the flow of traffic. I know how to embark and disembark ferry boats, shift down when going over mountain passes and cruise in and out of Canada, smiling and making eye contact with the border patrol.

But on the Big Island, I like to mainly drive straight and turn right. You'd think by the way I avoid left turns that I just learned to drive yesterday. To get around Hilo, all anybody has to do is go straight and turn right or left but even *I* am amazed at what I do to avoid making a left turn. Sometimes I drive a whole 'nother block so I can get to where I'm going by taking a couple of right turns instead of one left.

Car behavior. Is there a cultural context? If so, what are the implications? If not, then what am I doing?

CHAPTER 8

DA KINE

On her recent visit to Hawai`i, my friend from Seattle asked me for the meaning of da kine. I was surprised because for all of her trips to Honolulu and Hilo, I never gave a thought to the possibility that she still hadn't picked up the meaning of da kine. We use it everywhere, anywhere, and it's even in the trademark of some island products and businesses. Anyone hanging around locals will surely hear it several times a day but no matter how often she runs into this phrase, it still baffles her. And she reminded me that I only say it in Seattle when I'm talking to other Hawai`i people but not to her so how was she supposed to learn it? She made a good point.

So I launched into it. "Well, da kine...it's whatever it is we're talking about... you know, da kine." For half of you out there, that's clear, right? But perhaps the other half will be glad that my Seattle friend said, "Examples please?"

So again I dove in. "Look, let's say I tell you, 'Eh, we go eat da kine.' It means you and I know exactly what it is that we're going to eat. You know what I mean and I know you know what I mean."

She looked at me puzzled. "No, you're wrong. I still don't know what you mean. In fact, I don't have a clue what you're talking about."

This was going to be trickier than I anticipated. But again in the name of friendship, I plowed on. "OK, suppose I say to you, 'You see dem ovah deah? Dey da kine you know.' You and I both know what it means."

But as I looked at her frowning, cloudy face, I could tell she wasn't following my explanations and it forced me to recall a chapter I read years ago in a linguistics book, a discussion of high versus low context speech environments.

When I'm engaged in local, island conversation, I am in a high context environment where we all understand what we're talking about, so fewer words are necessary. However, my friend and I know each other mainly in Seattle which for me is a low context environment where I'm required to use many words and detailed explanations, like this one. Verbose, convoluted and redundant describe most of my verbal engagements on the Mainlin which is why I don't care to talk much up there.

But here in Hawai`i, I'm happy to converse because my speech is sleek, streamlined and economical with the pristine clarity of Kealakekua Bay where I like to go, to watch all the da kine.

CHAPTER 9

CHECKS

I was on campus at the University of Hawai`i in Hilo walking be-hind some students who weren't local. How did I know they were not from the Islands? Many things but among them was this conversation:

"And people here won't let me pay for anything! Every time we go out together, they insist on paying!"

I thought about jumping in and shouting, "You're always sup-posed to fight for the check! And remember – when you win, you pay! So when you lose, you try to win next time! And in order to win, you have to try harder to get the check so you can pay!" But I knew they would just think I was a babbling, pupule old lady.

I know they're confused because I remember this same confu-sion in reverse when I first left the Islands to go to Seattle. It took me a while to figure out why nobody was fighting for the check because in Hawai`i when the check arrives at the table, everyone dives in to grab it and it often rips after a little tug of war. Sometimes it doesn't even get delivered when one of the diners leaves the table and sneaks to find the waitress, threatening to hold her hostage unless she lets him pay right now before their food is served. At the end of the meal when the waitress announces that the bill has been taken care of and the other adults realize they've been duped into not paying, they might throw wads of money that go fluttering across the table. The payer flings it back, the dupes shove it away, the payer dismisses it with a hand wave and so it goes. When this happens, the children stop playing to watch the flying dollars, eyes darting back and forth as if at a ping pong game. It ends only when someone concedes defeat and reluctantly stuffs the money back in their wallet, planning a strategy to make sure they get the check next time.

But I learned the hard way that this is not how it is done on the continent.

What I understood in those early days in Seattle was that others are not going to fight you to pay so if you dive for the check, you will surely get it. Instead, the waiter gently lays the bill on the table where it sits for so long that it starts to curl around the edges. No one looks at it and I swear it's growing mold before somebody finally gingerly picks it up with two fingers and reluctantly turns it over, taking care to not let it touch other parts of the body. At this point, everyone notices it as if for the first time. "Oh, the check... is that the check? The check's here...let's take care of the check."

From here on, there are several options:

"OK, what's the total? Let's just split it evenly six ways" (or however many diners there are.) This is the most generous offer. But what if I only had the salad and you had the steak? So then somebody has to say, "But you only had the salad and I had the steak. So here's my amount for the steak."

Unfortunately, this doesn't always happen and the steak eater runs a risk whenever he or she doesn't offer to pay their share because the others will start to notice and eventually talk.

So the safest option is "OK, you had the salad so that's $6.75 and you had half a turkey sandwich with soup - $8.50, and you had the steak – that's twelve and a quarter... wait, who had the beer? Add two ninety-five. The ice cream...?" and so on. You get the picture. We even split for the tip.

If you're in education and reading the kinds of reports that I have to read about student outcomes, you would have to wonder how come Americans aren't scoring way up there in math with all the arithmetic that takes place in restaurants.

I think I like the Hawai`i way better where we take turns winning.

CHAPTER 10

BASICS

There's a lot of talk about going back to basics so here's my take: I used to have a coffee table in my living room in Seattle, in front of the sofa. Then one day I asked myself what is that long, rectangular piece of dead wood doing, taking up important space and blocking the path to the couch? It was like a speed bump that forced me to slow down and even so, I was still in imminent danger of crashing into one of its sharp corners.

After several bruising encounters, I started assessing the purpose of this bulky piece of furniture. Why this low table upon which I feel compelled to park a stoneware bowl, a porcelain figurine, that wire sculpture from the craft fair? And why do we call it a *coffee* table? Do tea drinkers have a tea table? While I was often tempted to put my coffee cup down on this table, I usually didn't, ever mindful of creating water marks which would then increase the amount of housework to avoid. And did I mention the dust that gathered on this table although sometimes I was able to convince myself that it was art, like the delicate, swirling patterns of lint left by that crocheted doily, for example.

Then I saw how magazines and newspapers liked to pile up on this piece of furniture. So maybe I should be calling it the magazine table but wait. Why not just organize my reading material in the magazine rack? I can't put my coffee there so why do I put magazines on the coffee table?

And I started to notice that when we sat on the sofa, we put our feet up on the coffee table which cannot be good for the coffee nor the table. So why not call it a foot table? Except that I have a footstool for feet. Can I put my coffee on the footstool? No, only feet although an occasional newspaper did find its way to the footstool and sometimes stayed for days.

I finally got rid of that coffee table and oh, the space! My living room feels like the open range where we can freely roam with neither menacing speed bumps nor pesky reminders to dust. Now I'm looking at the other furniture. What about that side table with the lamp and potted plant? I could get rid of it, replace the table lamp with a floor model and put the plant elsewhere. But now that the kids are on their own, why am I giving myself one more thing to feed and take care of? Besides, I spend a lot of time in Hawai`i where plants can show up uninvited at the house, creep up the stairs and seductively twist themselves around railings if you don't cut them back so I'll satisfy any botanical yearnings there. The bookcase stores some once- (or never-) read books as well as lacquer and glass tadaksh, begging for more dusting. Exactly why am I holding on to them? And come to think of it, I often find myself sitting on the floor so tell me again why I need this sofa, especially since it is usually used for napping. But there's a bed in the bedroom for that so why...?

Basics. I'm going back.

CHAPTER 11

CRACK SEED

Every now and then someone tries to correct my oral English. I've even been told that I speak English... *almost* like a native speaker. To which I reply, "Eh... you too! Your English not so bad. Not so good but, not so bad."

My friend Bill from Hilo told me that the first time he went to California, someone remarked that he spoke with an accent. "Which was funny," Bill said, "because I thought she was the one with the accent."

In one of the Honolulu newspapers, I was reading about my favorite snack crack seed which are dried plums, peaches and apricots that have been Chinese-spiced then left to soak in crocks or glass jars. The fruit pit is cracked so it can collect the sticky juice from the sauce that forms and this is how it stands out as an island treat. Once we start sucking on the delicious ooze hiding in the seed's crevices, the flavor seems to never end but right when we think we've sucked it dry and are ready to spit out the pieces, our taste buds are surprised with another final burst of `onoliciousness.

But I'm getting sidetracked remembering my favorite snack so let's go back to the newspaper. In the middle of the article, the writer scolded us locals for saying "crack seed," pontificating that it should be pronounced *cracked* seed, not crack seed.

Look, as an English teacher I know a few things about the English language and can tell you that what the newspaper writer wants us to use is a participial adjective but I have neither time nor inclination to give you all the gory grammar details.

Furthermore, being instructed to say cracked seed instead of crack seed reminds me of a similar scolding about shave ice. "That should be *shaved* ice," I was once informed by the language police, making the same point about the way we like to drop the –ed at the end of the participial adjective. (There it is again but you'll just have to fire up your computer search engine.) Sometimes I even see a shop selling our cool and icy after-beach snack, run by people who have either been beaten up by the grammar cops or are themselves members of the grammar regulatory commission. But as a personal protest, whenever I see a sign announcing *Shaved Ice*, I walk away no matter how `ono I am for a large lime-li hing mui-liliko`i. How good can it be if they caved in to the English grammar mafia? It's *Shave Ice* and if you're from Hilo, *Ice Shave*. Don't try to talk me out of it.

So let me challenge all you insistent English speakers out there to a smack down with this opening qualifying question: Explain in twenty-five words or less *why* grammar books instruct us to say crack<u>ed</u> seed and shav<u>ed</u> ice.

And if you get past that one, here's the follow up: Kindly enumerate why someone of my ilk, who knows the rules of English grammar, will always take pleasure in saying *crack seed* and *shave ice*.

And to all who have been trying unsuccessfully for decades to convert me to using only textbook English, I have these two words for you to think about: ice cream. I'll bet a hundred dollars that in my lifetime and yours, we are never going to hear anybody ever say *iced* cream.

I rest my case.

CHAPTER 12

HONEY

I was going through the checkout at a supermarket in Seattle when a brash, young cashier called me dear. Dear?! As in: Here's your change, dear.

When did I become a dear? For years I was a honey, especially at coffee shops and doctors' offices around Puget Sound where I suppose so many people go through in a day that no one on the staff can possibly remember all the names, unless they tried of course. And perhaps there are some among us who enjoy being called "Honey" but I am not one of them although I'm still trying to decide if Honey is better than "you there with lipstick on your teeth." I'm leaning toward "you there."

When I hear Honey, I know these folks not only do not know my name but aren't going to bother learning it. I will not be fooled by "Darlin'" either because that's just Honey from the South. Not only that, anyone with honey dripping from their lips is usually one small step away from ignoring the said Honey. How hard do you have to work to get a refill on your coffee from the waitress who just called you Honey?

It's true that sometimes I myself use the term honey but only when I'm being flippant and trying to make a point, as in "you better believe it Honey." And I only say this to people I know quite intimately, never to strangers.

My suspicions about Honey go back to when I was in college in Seattle and warily wading into the world of dating. I immediately went on guard when a maybe boyfriend called me Honey or Cutie or Sweetie. If that was supposed to be a compliment, thank you very much but it put me on shaky ground. Was I supposed to respond in kind and can't I just call him by his name? I finally deduced that when one of these endearments left the lips of the now maybe not boyfriend, it was probably because he had so many honeys and cuties out there that he didn't remember exactly which one he was with and could not risk the wrong name. He was covering `ōkole and that was the kiss of death, so aloha and adios Sweetie.

Now that I've moved way past the era of young bucks and have entered the age of old goats, I'm hearing these terms everywhere. But I am still not fooled by this fake cloak of loving and caring. I know there's something sinister about such false intimacy. But to add insult to injury, I've graduated to Dear and we all know what that means: not just Honey, but *old* Honey. Look, I don't mind getting older but there is no need to make public service announcements.

Instead of Dear, Honey or Sweetie, I wish others would adopt our custom in Hawai`i where we call each other by name or sometimes Braddah, Sistah, Cuz, and everyone in the older generation is Auntie and Uncle. That is so much nicer and who wouldn't prefer feeling like part of the family rather than one step away from being shipped out to the old folks home.

So please, call me Auntie OK? No really, I insist. Just don't honey me my dear.

CHAPTER 13

HUMUHUMUNUKUNUKUAPUA`A

I like to watch fish but in Seattle, I can't bear to watch these noble creatures laid out as if they were decorator tiles, stiff and cold at Pike Place Market. Sometimes they get unceremoniously tossed from their ice bed to the weighing scale as part of entertainment. I am not entertained and I don't like it. Or else I can watch fish in aquariums at office waiting rooms but I wonder if they feel claustrophobic, swimming around and around the small tanks. I am never surprised when one of them tries to jump out. I would too.

So fish-watching is not something I do in Seattle but in Hawai`i, it is one of my favorite ocean activities although lately, I've been thinking more about it.

On a trip back to the Big Island, I went with one of my boys to Kealakekua Bay and as we swam a ways out, we saw the sea floor drop off sharply and disappear from view. My son and I came up for air, gasping with surprise.

"Let's head back to shore," I said. "You don't know *what* you might see way down there in the deep."

"Or," my boy countered," what might see *you*."

Not wanting to lose our place on the food chain, we splashed back to land as fast as our feet could flap the water. A little respect for these ocean inhabitants is important. Let me tell you more.

I was snorkeling on the Kona side of the island. What could be more relaxing than following little fishies around, watching them glide then dart in and out of tiny coral caves? At least what's what I used to think until I ran into a humuhumunukunukuāpua`a. This in itself is not unusual; there are many humuhumunukunukuāpua`a in those waters. But this humuhumu was lining up straight out in front of me, making eye contact as he wiggled his tail, then charged right at my face mask. Just before crashing into it he veered off to the side, circled back into confrontational position, eye contact, tail wiggle, then charged again! In disbelief I watched him do this several times before I finally swam back to shore, wondering what was the reef fish world coming to. Here was a gentle triggerfish whose name was longer than it was, trying to attack something that could easily squash him.

But it made me think that maybe the fish are fed up with us blockers of sunlight with one large glassy eye, false gift-bearers of small peas that turn fish flesh green, ruthless coral killers carelessly trampling on their home. Perhaps they're revolting against mysterious nets scooping up friends and family to be sold off and doomed to confinement and isolation in pet shops and aquariums.

Could it be that they are protesting our human invasion of their coral reef?

So don't laugh next time a snorkeler reports dive-bombing by an angelfish or face-slapping from a butterfly fish. That attack-humu might be the result of some errant mutant gene or maybe human behavior is changing the world around the reef. Whichever it is, just remember that with my one glassy eye, I actually saw this little humuhumunukunukuāpua`a trying to fend off an invader.

And he must be much bigger now.

CHAPTER 14

EDUCATION

When I was growing up in Hilo, I had to devise ways to navigate American education which arrived shortly after 1898 with the annexation of Hawai`i to the United States. This new system prohibited the Hawaiian language in public schools which is the reason why we islanders today speak such good English but not much Hawaiian.

In case you're thinking I must have been around in 1898, the answer is no but my elementary school years still go back far enough to a time when most of the teachers were haole from the Mainlin. They looked and talked different from us and spoke of exotic far-away places like Michigan and Ohio. They did things in strange ways and I clearly remember the day I discovered that if I looked directly at Miss Olive when she was asking a question, she glanced at me, smiled then looked away. This was stunning since outside of school, I knew to *not* look directly at any adult when they were talking to me. This was especially true when they were scolding or else I would have to confess to a priest that I sassed. While my mother went on and on about some petty sin I had committed, I had to stand with hands behind my back, properly contrite and looking down. Heaven help us all if I put even one hand on my hip or looked up at her. And forget about saying a word to defend myself because if I did, all hell would break loose.

But I slowly realized that this was not how it went in school with Miss Olive from Indiana so I continuously tested my theory, brazenly looking at each teacher when she talked and sure enough, nine times out of ten she didn't call on me but roamed around the room looking for somebody else, settling usually on the braddah with his head down and eyes glued to the floor. Was he being polite or didn't have the answer? I don't know but felt safe because I was working the eye thing.

I tried to tell some friends about my discovery but they didn't want to chance it so for a while I had this little gem all to myself. After all, since the teacher didn't call on me when I looked at her, what would happen if suddenly everybody in class started looking her straight in the eye? There was one drawback when occasionally, a teacher in a rush to get the answer would call on the student looking up at her - me - and I would get caught in my own smug and secret web.

"Who wrote the Rime of the Ancient Mariner...ummmm... Rochelle?"

Scrambling like crazy, I then developed the skill to bluff my way through, so I was going to try Shakespeare which was always a good guess with these kinds of questions.

"Ahhhhh...I think his name begins with Ssss..."

"Correct!" shouted the teacher in a hurry. "Ssssamuel...Taylor Coleridge."

See? That's how we got so smart. But the thing about education is that you never quite know how new-found knowledge will be applied and in Hawai`i, the answer might be Las Vegas, the gambling Mecca so often visited and even resettled by islanders that it is sometimes called the Ninth Hawaiian Island.

It could be that after more than a century of American education, we learned only too well how to bluff and play the odds.

Sounds plausible to me.

CHAPTER 15

FREE FUN

The Pacific Northwest is The Great Outdoors with all of those mountains, forests, rivers and lakes. But someone forgot to tell us before we packed up the children and left Hawai`i to move to Seattle, about the high cost of the great outdoors.

For example, you can't just drop a line in the water to go fishing; you need to buy a license first. And wait! You need one license for salmon, another for steelhead, yet another for sturgeon, all of which are different from the license for shellfish. You should probably also get some long rubber boots so your legs don't freeze off in the icy waters of the ocean, river or lake, even during the summer months. Which makes swimming not such an attractive choice either unless you want to invest in a wet suit and what's the fun in swimming wrapped up tight like a rubber band? The mountains are perfect for hiking and skiing but you need a loan from the bank to buy equipment for those beckoning outdoor sports.

Of course I can and have taken the children to public parks but the climate doesn't make this an option for the entire twelve months out of the year. Besides, by the time they're four, they're a little bored with the swings and the slide. By the time they're four, *I'm* a little bored watching them on the see-saw, going up and down, up and down.

"Let's go to Seattle Center," I offer and they cheer. But when we get there, I'm paying six bucks to park, five dollars apiece for entrance to the Children's Museum, three-fifty for a Belgian waffle at the Food Court, and one ninety-five for each of them to take a three-minute ride on the bumper cars at the Fun Forest. You do the math.

No wonder I'm willing to shell over hundreds of dollars to bring those kids back to Hilo. We can spend the entire day on the beach at Onekahakaha, scooping sand, netting small fish, chasing crab, squealing at sea cucumber, overturning shells and bobbing in the warm water. It costs me a cooler of juice, a pot of rice and a can of pork and beans. Because I still got money in my pocket at the end of the day, we stop for ice shave on the way home. I tell them, "Go ahead, order the rainbow! Get the deluxe with azuki beans or ice cream…better yet, take both!" I figure that even with the airfare, I'm still coming out way ahead. Everyone complains about the high cost of living in the Islands but I balance it out with the low cost of fun.

There are many reasons why I bring children home to Hawai`i every chance I have; this is only one of them.

CHAPTER 16

MISS UNIVERSE

Do you recall some years ago when Miss Universe was told to lose weight or lose her crown? I'm not making this up because the news story jumped out and bit me on my fat ʻōkole so I remember it well. After the dust-up, pageant officials denied the report but I was huffing, puffing, fuming, hissing and my main recourse when this happens is to light up my laptop to cook some comebacks.

Who decided that skinny was beautiful? Sunken cheeks, pointy elbows, skeletal spine bones running down the back like fish before it's been fillet-ed – not a pretty sight. But Miss Universe pageant officials aren't asking for my opinion although they should because I'm not the only one who thinks this way. I teach students from other countries and recently, one of them greeted me cheerfully in the hall with "Good morning. You're looking fat today!"

Some of you out there might have been offended but not me. After all my years of teaching, I knew this was a compliment. "Why thank you!" I beamed, basking in the confirmation that dinner the night before of two heaping bowls of beef stew and rice, kimchee on the side and strawberry ice cream for dessert was the right decision. Students say the nicest things, especially when they come from countries where having enough food to eat on a daily basis is an accomplishment. But I made a mental note to talk later in class about acceptable and unacceptable compliments in the U.S.

Even though Pacific islanders are by nature well-built, this thin-is-in notion has been floating around Hawai`i for at least a century. Before that, images of Hawaiian queens and other ali`i show graceful women of ample proportions. But nowadays, movies, magazines and television dictate which role models to follow and none of them look like the ali`i anymore.

When I was growing up in Hilo, once a year I went with my friends to the Miss Aloha Hawaii pageant. The winner would then compete in Honolulu for the title of Miss Hawaii which would lead to a one-in-fifty chance of being named Miss America. The Hilo contest was held at the old Armory by Wailuku River and women usually wore too much makeup that night, including those of us who were not contestants. And all of us overly-made-up girls sucked in our stomach trying to be tall, skinny, pale and long-legged.

So it makes me happy these days in Hilo to read about the Ms Aloha Nui contest that takes place every September. It began a few years ago during Aloha Week Festivals and was at first called Ms BIG Big Island. Women under the weight of 200 lbs need not apply thank you.

The Aloha Week Official Program states, "In Hawaiian culture and tradition, the larger the woman, the more beautiful and queenly she was considered. Big women were revered."

I think I'll send a copy of this program to Miss Universe pageant officials to remind them that in some places, the extra pounds on their beauty queen make her even more gorgeous. And then, I'm going to tell that former Miss Universe to come to the Big Island where she'll always be a winner.

At least I hope so.

CHAPTER 17

SLEEP

I'm a sleeper. But if you're thinking of a dark horse winning the big race or an indie movie making it to the megaplex, the answer is no. I'm not that kind of a sleeper. I'm the other kind. I love to sleep. In fact, I'm a big sleeper. Not only do I love to sleep, I sleep as much as I can. My friends know not to call me after 9pm because even if I'm still awake, my brain is shutting down and they might as well be talking to the cat.

What's more, I figured out over the years how to sleep with my eyes open. I perfected this practice in school, taking short naps as the teacher blathered about the Crimean War or Picasso's Blue period. I learned how to prop a hand under my chin with elbow resting on the desk so that my head angled intelligently, inquiringly. But once during a lecture on Australopithecus and others of his ilk, my elbow slipped and my head fell with a thud on the desk top. With eyes wide open, you'd think I'd have seen that coming. But that didn't cure me of napping, only of propping my head with my hand on tiny folding desks. And now that I'm on the other end of the classroom dissecting passive voice and dangling modifiers, I can easily spot those students who are sleeping with their eyes open and it makes me want to...give them extra credit!

It isn't universally accepted that sleep is a good thing. When I arrived in Seattle for college, I met students who bragged about not needing any sleep at all. Even now I hear about folks who can get by on just three hours and I wonder what universe they're from. Perhaps the same one as Benjamin Franklin who said "Waste not life. In the grave will be sleeping enough." Good ole Ben. I don't always take his advice but there is one lesson from him that's useful in Hilo: Don't fly your kite in the rain.

Now finally, I think more people are getting in touch with their sleepy side. One recent study shows that sleep helps you lose weight which in my opinion is common sense. You're usually not eating if you're sleeping. And big companies, recognizing nowadays that sleep recharges the brain and increases productivity, are providing energy pods for their employees to nap in the office. In New York City is a business where you can pay 14 bucks for a 20-minute snooze on your break from work.

My advice? Forget the pods and pay-for-naps. Just put your head on the desk for a quick doze. Tell them Auntie said. And if you can't lay your head down because you're in class or at a meeting where nothing useful or helpful is being discussed, practice napping with your eyes open. Just be sure your arm is on a stable surface when it is propping up your chin.

CHAPTER 18

AINOKEA

I have to admit to you that in Seattle, I always seem to be half a step off the fashion dictates of the times. Some might even say I am a whole step off but one reason is that I can never keep up with it and the other reason is: Ainokea. When I was growing up in Hilo in the days before television and jet airplanes, it took fashion fads two years to make the boat crossing from the West Coast to Honolulu then another six months before they came to Hilo. It is no wonder I am so far behind the current styles.

Even when I try to figure out what's hot and what's not, I don't get it. Matching prints and colors especially confounds me. I've noticed that in Seattle, I can't put on my yellow palaka blouse, pink beaded sweater and red flowered skirt to go out without strangers walking wide swaths around me, sometimes crossing the street as I approach.

But in Hilo when I was a teenager, I once sought the fashion advice of one of my aunties to ask if I could wear this shiny purple top with those bright green printed pants.

"Look" Auntie said, "all around you. Every color and texture you can imagine are on flowers blooming in between green leaves. Aren't they all beautiful? And show me *one* that doesn't match." Then she gave me her blessing on my fine outfit.

So what about jewelry? If I like that necklace and this pin plus those earrings with matching bracelet and ring, who says I can't bedeck myself with all of them in one fell swoop? Especially if I'm wearing red, pink, yellow, green and purple flowers and plaids, surely something would match.

As you can tell by now, the reason why in Seattle I'm usually off step is because when it comes to clothing, looking stylish is nowhere on my list. I am never even sure what that means. And while it's true that ainokea much about what I wear, I'm not entirely without standards. For example, sweaters should be warm and washable; tops must have a cottony-feel, and pants need an elastic waistband. Socks cannot be too tight at the top ribbing and shoes must rest firmly on the ground. Open heel and open toe are best although not at the same time except in the summer. Hats should be snug in order to stay on gusty days and not so wide-brimmed to lift me off like the Flying Nun.

Sometimes I see people in Seattle and know they're from Hawai`i. Maybe it's the short-sleeve aloha shirt they're wearing with shorts and rubber slippahs on a blustery 50° Northwest day. Or perhaps it's the jacket that doesn't quite fit because it's been in the closet for months, maybe years and only sees daylight when it gets taken out for trans-ocean trips.

But then, I also notice people in Hawai`i who are far outside the local fashion groove if there is such a thing. Exhibit A would have to be mu`umu`u with tennis shoes, followed closely by shirt tucked into shorts with ankle socks and loafers. I also see that other dead give-away not-from-the-Islands make-up trick: nose painted in a white triangle. I never know if this is body protection, beautification or war paint.

So my fashion advice is this: Ainokea. Whatever works for you, works for me.

CHAPTER 19

OLYMPICS

Every two years when the Olympics Games start up, a question pops into my head: Who decides which sports should be Olympic events? I can understand some that come from ancient Greece like discus or javelin, but air gun? What about that one where an athlete cross-country skis then takes out his rifle and shoots at a stationary target. Takes more skill to hike Mauna Kea hunt wild pig.

A few years ago, I heard about a new winter event called curling, a word I used to associate with hair. I'll assume then that the players are called curlers. And during the last Summer Olympics as I watched world-class high divers, I couldn't help but wonder who determined that bouncing on the board resulted in deductions or that the smaller the splash, the greater the score?

Who decides things like which new sport to introduce and how to recognize a winner at the Olympic Games and how come nobody asks me?

I was at Coconut Island one sunny day in Hilo. There's a lava rock tower built in the 1920s on this small island in the bay that in olden days was called Moku`ola, and one of life's pleasures growing up in Hilo is jumping off the Coconut Island tower.

Go there if you want to see gold medal water athletes. However, you will rarely see anyone diving from the tower because jumping seems to be the main event. I remember when we jumped from the Coconut Island tower, we yelled "Bombs Away!" And everyone who jumps into the ocean tries to make the biggest splash. But the size of the splash is not necessarily correlated to the size of the jumper. Technique counts – jumping curled up into a ball; jumping straight in then bending your knees right before hitting the water, jumping high then flipping backwards, or wiggling your legs, or landing `ōkole first.

Nowadays there's ice dancing, canoe slalom and trampoline in the Games so there's got to be an Olympic event in the Coconut Island tower jump. Who can deny the artistry and precision required in jumping off a tower with hands and feet pointing downward then twisting and twirling in order to hit the water butt first?

So I propose to the Olympics committee, a new sport: High Tower Jumping, where the biggest splash gets the most cheers and for which I will volunteer to set the standards, devise the point system and describe the award-winning moves. I will also be happy to serve as one of the judges.

I guarantee that this will be the event where Coconut Islanders bring home the gold.

CHAPTER 20

ELECTIONS

I t wasn't so long ago that whenever strangers knocked on my mother's door in Hilo to give her an orchid, it was a sign that this was an election year. Other campaign artifacts lying around the house were combs, letter openers, pencils, pens and paper fans, all inscribed with the name of a candidate.

But during elections around Puget Sound, nobody gives me anything and the only time someone knocks on my door is when they want permission to put their candidate's sign up in our yard. I have to give it some serious thought because all my neighbors who barely know my name will now know my political inclinations.

. In Hawai`i, we're proud of our tradition of carrying signs and waving to cars at busy intersections right before elections. Candidates and supporters in Seattle do this too on frigid, rainy November days, bundled up in parkas and ski caps, stomping their hiking boots to keep the blood circulating, waving gloved hands during the semi-dark morning and evening commutes.

This I see as proof that some good ideas from the Islands should not cross the ocean.

But waving signs at major traffic intersections is not what used to set island elections apart. It was the orchids. Or refrigerator magnets, or memo clipboards, or snack packs of dried fruit. Small gifts – that's how the vote got out on the Big Island, although there was always one candidate who got carried away.

Once when I arrived in Hilo a few weeks before elections, my mother had on her lanai an unopened hydroponic lettuce kit which included a plastic quart container with lid, fertilizer packet, cotton balls, a plastic forestry tube and lettuce seeds. All of this came compliments of the candidate with the campaign promise: *Let's grow together.*

When Mom invited me to grow the lettuce hydroponically, the English teacher in me guessed that it had something to do with water but that was all I knew. I peered in, examined the kit but decided to pass. Sorry Mr. Politician, you'll just have to grow it alone while I go to the Farmer's Market and *buy* some lettuce.

But when the orchid plant arrived, it was a stroke of genius! A potholder is nice but the orchid had everybody talking. *You got one? How big yours? And what, healthy? Was blooming??*

These were some of the conversations I heard in Hilo right before election time.

But wait. "What about the candidate's platform?" I asked Mom.

"Yeah," she replied. "I going ask about that because I got so many orchids crowding under the lychee tree, I could use one of those platforms."

My mother tells me things are changing in Hilo and she hasn't gotten any gifts this election year. Too bad I say.

CHAPTER 21

PERFUME

Once I had to fly on a packed plane from Seattle to Honolulu, sitting the whole time next to someone who must have doused herself with half a bottle of perfume. I don't know what kind of perfume it was but from the looks of this utterly stylish woman, I'm sure it was very expensive perfume. Still, expensive or cheap, it didn't matter because I got sick. In a confined space like an airplane, I can't even stand a faint scent of brewed coffee let alone the stench of what my nose identifies as rotting fruit and dead flowers. It was a very long flight home and my seatmate was lucky I didn't barf on her exquisite purple velour pantsuit.

Perfume experts want to know what type am I: Woodsy Outdoors... Romantic Floral...Fresh Mountain Air? If they only knew that the correct answers are Raw Fish, Sweating Horses, Coconut Oil. And these days when both females *and* males over-spray themselves, the only good thing about someone wearing their signature scent is you can smell them coming. The boss enters the room behind me and my olfactories start flashing red. Quick! Say something brilliant!

Go to the big department stores in Seattle and be prepared for perfume salespeople urging you to try their company's latest product. I detour around the entire make-up section just to avoid those spritzers. Imagine if I stuck a blooming plumeria branch under your nose. Here! Smell this now! You will like it!

I'm careful to not cross paths with those storm troopers of stink.

And yet there are certain smells others complain about that never bother me. A whiff of the dried shrimp, fish and salted turnips from open bins in Chinatown markets brings back happy memories of shopping with my grandmother. The distinct aroma of ʻōpū simmering for hours on the stove means Dad's famous tripe stew for dinner. When I cook harm ha pork in Seattle, neighbors might jump in their car and speed off, but all the flies in the neighborhood make their way to my house, throwing themselves on our window screen to breathe deeply the emissions from the exhaust fan. They know the good stuff.

And what about kim chee? My family can't get enough of the spicy and sublime condiment in various cabbage and cucumber forms. After a mouthful, we like to ask each other, "Hhhhow's the kimchee?"…just to make sure that no one is left outside of the circle of sensuous and seductive smells.

So that gives me this idea. If we're going to continue to rub artificial odors on our body, let's expand the list of offerings and I might get interested. Midnight in Monaco is OK, but what about Midnight on Mamo Street? If Black Pearl is so evocative, why not Black Bean? Enticed by Evening in Paris? I'll take Afternoon at the Wharf. You like Wild Strawberry? I pick Sour Lemon. You say Wind Song? I choose Salt Air.

Maybe before my next plane ride, I should dab some Pink Bagoong behind my ears. It just might offset the Blue Gardenia emanating from my seatmate.

CHAPTER 22

PAST TENSE

My work and pleasure for over twenty-five years has been teaching English to students from other countries. And while I help them maneuver the mysterious maze we call English grammar and syntax, they in turn help me understand some of the vagaries of life. Here is an example.

One week in class, we were practicing the past tense forms of irregular verbs: drink-drank, teach-taught, see-saw. On that Monday morning, I asked them, "What did you do this past weekend?" And students dutifully answered: *I went to a movie; I made chicken; I took my son to the park;* and so on. Yes, yes, I nodded encouragingly. Good, good, I continued in my teacherly talk.

But then, one student said, "I bought an iPhone on Amazon." Wow...I was impressed but so was the rest of the class. And now various verbs and tenses were flying all over the room. *How much you pay? What you got on it? How to spell Amazon?"*

Conversation was flowing with ease as students discussed this latest toy in technology. A few pulled out their old cell phones and iPods to show each other. Some were even remembering to use the past tense! This kind of interaction is the stuff of language teachers' dreams and I leaned back against the desk to revel in it. But no sooner was I congratulating myself with great satisfaction when a dark cloud began to gather over my English teacher's brain. Here were students, discussing the newest technology – one just purchased the latest gadget via his computer – and I'm worrying about the past tense of irregular verbs? Who cares if anyone says: *Yesterday I bought an iPhone on Amazon* or *yesterday I buy an iPhone on Amazon.* The heart of the matter is that someone had enough cyber-sophistication to procure an iPhone on the Internet. Message sent and received; correct usage of past tense is irrelevant.

I understand this because in Pidgin, the language from Hawai`i that I love to wallow in when I am not teaching American English to unsuspecting students, we don't worry about past tense either and in fact, there's really only one past tense form: *wen.* As in *What you wen do yestahday? How much fish you wen catch?* We don't worry about regular or irregular verbs: swim-swam, eat-ate, drive-drove. But not only tense; we often gleefully and flagrantly ignore the almighty BE verb: *How you? You teacha?* And come to think of it, we also don't pay much attention to prepositions. Either we use it wrong: *He stay play music on top da radjo.* Or we drop it completely: *Like go beach?*

So, in order to function in one of the worlds I inhabit, no need tense, no need preposition, sometimes no need verb even.

Ey, maybe no need English teacha!

CHAPTER 23

RICE

I love rice. Hot, cold, fresh, old, plain, fried, gravied, nori'd – you name it, I'll eat it.

The first time I had to be away from my rice was when I left Hawai`i to go to school in the Pacific Northwest in the 1960s. College menus back then offered standard American fare - meatloaf, fried chicken, potatoes, peas and carrots - not the cornucopia of foods-from-around-the-world found on campuses today. In the 60s, we either ate in the dorm cafeteria or in the dorm dining room. Every evening we joined the house mother who supervised us at a sit-down dinner in case we had arrived at the university without knowing how to sup quietly, converse politely or wield a knife and fork. We didn't find any rice but instead, bread, pasta and potatoes – mashed, fried, baked, hashed, stuffed, boiled...

Nowadays when Hawai`i students arrive at the U, they bring an automatic rice cooker as one of their necessities but those didn't exist back in my day and by the middle of the first fall quarter in Seattle, my beloved rice was a fading memory. Finally when all the trees on campus had lost their leaves, we saw rice on the menu. Word spread like fast-moving lava, lighting up dark recesses and igniting small fires in the homesick hearts of all us Hawai`i students.

Best of all, the rice was on the breakfast menu which meant we wouldn't have to wait until lunch or dinner and forced to wile away the hours daydreaming in poetry class (How do I love rice? Let me count the ways...) or in History (What year was the War of the Rices?) or in Philosophy (Why rice?)

We locals made big plans the night before to get up extra early to spend more time at breakfast. I even set my hair. The next morning, alarms went off and we jumped out of bed, washed, brushed then dressed and hurried down to the cafeteria, reminiscing about our favorite breakfast dishes: fried rice with char siu and green onion; two scoop rice with a couple of eggs on top, sunny-side up; rice with scrambled eggs, Portuguese sausage on the side.

When we turned the corner to the cafeteria, we picked up trays and utensils and slid them on the round metal pipes. But as we got closer to the food, we fell silent and slowed down. Looking up ahead, it was hard to believe what our eyes were seeing. The cafeteria servers set down bowls of steaming, shiny, pearly rice over which non-Hawai`i students were adding...sugar and milk!

We looked back and forth at each other, eyes wide and mouth open. Whoever heard of rice with milk and sugar? Is that how we're supposed to eat it up here? We should have just forged ahead to pick up a bowlful along with some scrambled eggs and bacon but there was something unnatural about the sight of milked and sugared rice that spoiled our appetite. Feeling slightly queasy and a little dizzy, we put back the utensils and trays and left in silence. Gloom hung overhead like a big, black umbrella and no rice was eaten that day. We had gotten so close, only to have it slip away. O elusive starch!

Back in the days when going away to college was like going to the moon, it's a miracle that any of us graduated.

CHAPTER 24

EXERCISE

In Seattle occasionally and always by mistake, I surf by those exercise programs on TV where buff bodies are aerobicizing and encouraging you to keep up.

"C'mon and join us! You can do it!" they insist, flashing perfect teeth and pumping finely-toned arms and legs.

I stop to watch when the setting is a beach, which it often is. I find these programs mildly entertaining and am particularly intrigued at the way some people can look so good when they exercise and break neither a sweat nor train of thought nor stream of words. I'm also admiring the backdrop of glistening white sand laced with gentle foam from the blue blue ocean but wondering why anyone doesn't just jump in the water and go for a swim, if they're so eager for exercise.

Then there's all the equipment you can purchase so that in the safety of your family room, you can bicycle twenty miles, power walk up and down two thousand stairs, cross-country ski and row your boat. On TV commercials, the aerobic rider or walk meister is always in a sparse room with gleaming wooden floors and tall windows. And the scenery! Behind those sparkling windows (which I always wonder who cleans,) you can see the forest or the mountains on a clear and cloudless day. Am I the only one who thinks why spend $300 on a machine, or even $79.95 on a lycra body suit and leggings? Why not just put on your old sweats with the puka shirt to go outside for a walk and breathe in the crisp, fresh air.

I know people who are religious about their daily stroll along Puget Sound but in order to accomplish their exercise routine, they drive miles to arrive at their favorite walking spot. I see dedicated joggers in perpetual training for the next marathon, taking their car to the automated carwash.

I'm confused.

My friend in Hawai`i says that when her children beg her to join the gym so they can bench press while admiring themselves in the wall-to-wall mirror, she tells them "You wanna work out? Mop my floor! Or better yet, go cut Auntie's grass!"

I confess I am not immune to the fitness craze but because I travel regularly between Seattle and Hilo, I'm still trying to factor in variables such as seasons and climate. I admit that as I get older and move up to the front line facing mortality, I think more and more about exercising. In fact, I've made a vow to increase everyday the amount of time I devote to thinking about exercise. Today I thought about it for five minutes. Tomorrow I'll try to think about it for ten.

In the meantime, I got weeds to pull.

CHAPTER 25

SWIMSUIT

I bought a new swimsuit in Seattle before I came home to the Big Island. It was bright blue with big white flowers, bust lifter, optional straps, and "for the mature figure," a tummy-slimming panel in front. "Hmmmmm..." I thought as I checked my mature figure in the dressing room mirror. "OK and half price too. I can live with this."

But all I needed was to go for a swim on the first hot day back in Hilo to know I had made a big mistake. Looking around, I remembered that locals never wear bright blue swimsuits with white flowers...strapless with the tummy tuck panel. I must have been momentarily pupule when I forked over $22.50 in Seattle.

When am I going to learn that what looks good in the Pacific Northwest doesn't usually cross the ocean.

I was reminded of this again when I wore turquoise pedal pushers to ride horse in Hōlualoa. I wasn't planning to go horseback riding while packing in Seattle so when I got the invitation, quick I checked the closets and drawers in Hilo. About the only thing I had to ride horse in Kona were the pedal pushers which had been brought over from the West Coast who knows when but hanging untouched in the closet ever since. They were a little snug in the `ōkole but I still got into them even though my children wrinkled their nose in disgust.

"You're NOT wearing THAT are you?!"

Well yes in fact I am. Look. We're riding *horse* up Hualālai, not the Miss Hawaii *float* Kamehameha Day parade.

Imagine my surprise when halfway through the rainforest on horseback, the horse that had been gently ambling along next to me suddenly snapped and took a bite at the turquoise pants, leaving a clean, triangle-shaped rip near my knee. I figure he put up with it for as long as he could but just couldn't stand it any more. For the first time I realized how big horse teeth were but the amazing thing is that he didn't draw blood. It must have been just a warning and I decided right then and there that never mind if the kids don't like my clothes but when the animals object, I'd better pay attention.

Back in Hilo I remembered that sharks have been sighted out in open water. Sharks have sharp teeth and I thought about my new swimsuit from Seattle. Looking around the rocky shore, I noticed that most other local middle-aged women had on shorts and T-shirt and the few in swimsuit were wearing a one-piece black number with a large beach towel wrapped around their waist.

But I must have sensed something as soon as I landed on the island because my new blue suit with white flowers was safely stored away at my parents' house in Kaūmana, sales tag still on.

I walked to the ocean in my tight, faded black swimsuit, unwrapped the towel from where my waist used to be and carefully eased into the water.

Too bad my instincts let me down when I went horseback riding in Kona wearing turquoise pedal pushers.

CHAPTER 26

PLANT

I was reading a gardening column in a Seattle newspaper that was describing a plant with red flowers, purchased last summer which had refused to die this winter. The writer was wishing for a good, solid freeze to guarantee its demise.

"If only we could have some really cold weather," the gardener lamented, bemoaning the mild climate around Puget Sound. "Then we could really get it over with."

I heard the swoosh of the guillotine blade as it plummeted and landed on the delicate stalk of some nameless red flower which had the nerve not only to survive the winter but the gall to bloom! In case readers missed the point, the garden writer added "I wish it would die," and threatened to take action.

I took offense. For the first time in my life, I was forced to see the garden as a place of careless choices, thoughtless uprootings, rampant killings. "But it's a garden!" I said out loud to nobody in particular.

I always thought that everyone at least appreciated if not admired flowering plants until reading that column. This definitely was the downside of being literate. Imagine wishing for a cold snap in order to kill those tender and trusting seedlings you brought home from the nursery. And after they had kept their part of the bargain which was to grow and thrive, the only gratitude they got was the gardener praying for a frost to kill them off? Why not just rip out raging roots! Poison pesky petals...bazooka boastful blooms!!

You can see I'm a little upset here.

I remember the kwei-fa at the Lono Street house where I grew up in Hilo. The small tree looked fragile with thin branches that grew straight but it was tough with glossy dark green leaves and tiny, fragrant white flowers. One of my grandmothers planted it at the bottom of the front steps and every time we passed it on our way out, she broke off a blooming cluster and tucked it in her buttonhole so the sweet little flower came with us wherever we went, me and Apo.

My Portuguese grandmother planted another tree, a sturdy old variety of the yellow plumeria which provided flowers for lei the entire time we lived on Lono Street, not just for us and all our friends but for strangers passing by who would stop to ask if they could pick. When my parents sold the Lono Street house to build a new one, they took slips of the kwei-fa and plumeria to poke in the ground at Kaūmana for us to remember Apo and Cozy. Even today, family members break off branches to root and grow in their yard, keeping alive the memory of our grandmothers.

That gardening column in Seattle ended with plans to embark on a quest for another flower which the gardener promised not to kill.

But I don't believe her and I say we pull her planting permit.

CHAPTER 27

MENTAL

If you think I'm smart now, you should have known me when I was growing up in Hilo. But not just me; family and friends also became experts in mental gymnastics in order to make sense of what was in some of those books we were reading.

Plodding along on the wet side of a tropical island in the middle of the Pacific Ocean, I had to make meaning out of words like *prairie, blizzard, acorn,* moving on to *deciduous, contiguous, litigious.* There were endless foreign phrases to be learned. *Et tu Brute; Fourscore and seven years ago; O Blythe Spirit, bird thou never wert!* As for the mystical and magical sine and cosine, even today after scoring high enough on the math sections of the SATs and the GREs, I still wouldn't know a sine from a cosine if I ran one over on the Saddle Road.

Trying to be helpful, one of my aunties passed along her method of memory and recall. "When I have to remember something, I relate it to something else so bumbye I can make the connection," she told me. It seemed like a good idea until she later cautioned that perhaps her method wasn't dependable because the next time she met her new acquaintance Mr. Snow, she called him Mr. Flake. Still, these associations are worth a try and sometimes I use them.

The last time I was introduced to someone, I filed away – thank you Auntie - that his occupation began with an "a" so now I know that he is either a) an attorney b) an accountant c) an astronaut or d) an acrobat.

These are some of the skills I developed and carried to Seattle when I entered the University of Washington, continuing to memorize more phrases that would carry me through...the exam on the French Pluperfect for example. *Si j'avais su, je ne serai pas venue.* All I had to do was to plug in substitutions and voilà! I rummaged through other methodologies to remember obscure facts that I would later be asked to repeat: *olivine is always green; muscovite is always white*; moving on to graduate level *Derrida Deconstructs* and *Syntax is Chomsky*. Every now and again, a class came along based on such meaningless matter as "Aardvarks are clever snarks," and while classmates struggled mightily, I sailed right through, having spent my entire scholastic life offering proofs for such illogical nonsense.

I'm happy to report that I am in great company. Once on a family vacation to California, I nodded approvingly as my school teacher brother explained to my son that the best way to remember his hotel room number is to *take the War of 1812, subtract one, and then drop the first one.*

And a friend of mine who helps students pass citizenship classes tells them that they'll be able to name the original Thirteen Colonies if they would just connect them to the first letter of each word in the sentence **Coming directly (to) Georgia, my mother never never never never prayed religiously so vigorously.**

This is how we do it; that is why we are so smart.

CHAPTER 28

LADY

My mother tried to raise me to be a lady so that I wouldn't be a tita. She dressed me in pink pinafores edged in white lace, twirled my hair into ringlets and paid for piano lessons. She made me wear a rubber swim cap at the beach and asked Miss Gray at Hilo Library to steer me toward books that showed how to be a lady. But nothing moved me down the road to ladydom. I took scissors and cut my long hair before I got to kindergarten. At Onekahakaha Beach I swam out as far as I could then tore off the bathing cap, filled it with rocks and let it sink. I scoured the library stacks without Miss Gray to find my own unlady-like books. I practiced piano full of mistakes so that no one minded when I stopped playing, then crept down to the basement to chalk up a cue stick and sink balls into side pockets at my father's pool table.

Still, my mother kept trying and for most of my youth, I was surrounded by all of the trappings of ladyhood. But like clothes for the paper doll, some things just don't stick.

By the time I reached adolescence, I avoided pink and lace and let my hair do whatever it wanted. I had by then gotten some idea that ladies were supposed to smile sweetly, speak softly and walk lightly, and that nailed the lady coffin shut, since I liked to laugh loud with my mouth wide open all my teeth showing, shout out at my friends, and stomp around the house so the cockroaches know I'm home. Suffice it to say that any lingering, lady-like notions my mother had for me dissolved by the time I graduated from high school and I'm happy to report that I have been lady-free ever since.

In Seattle once, after a funeral of someone I clearly didn't know too well because she was being eulogized as "a lady," I marched right home and sat those three kids of mine down on the couch.

"Listen," I said, pointing my finger and running it in front of them. "I don't know which one of you will be delivering the eulogy at my funeral but whoever it is, don't be talking about me like I'm some *lady!*"

"As if," was their silent reply, eyes sliding back and forth at each other signaling that fo'real this time they had to send their madah to the pupule house. I know these looks; I've seen them before.

But all I was doing was giving those kids of mine fair warning that should this ill-advised word slip out at my funeral, I'll sit right up in my coffin to remind them one last time, that I ain't no lady!

CHAPTER 29

ENLIGHTENMENT

I believe that there are many paths to enlightenment and am currently pondering the one I saw at a storefront in a small town in Washington State that read: spirituality.com.

Growing up in Hilo, I went to confession on Saturday and attended Mass every Sunday at St. Joseph Catholic Church. I accompanied my Chinese grandmother to the graveyard for a Taoist ceremony that Apo called "paisan." I enjoyed Japanese bon dance with my Buddhist friends at the Hongwanji and followed Hawaiian warnings to carry ti-leaf over the Saddle Road.

I went to public school where we started every day reciting the *Pledge of Allegiance* followed by the *Our Father*, the Protestant version. The American Board of Christian Missions was the first to send missionaries from Boston to Hawai`i in 1820 so the Protestants had dibs. And right before the end of the prayer "...for Thine is the Kingdom..." etc., we Catholics were supposed to bite our tongue and close our ears because this was not in the Catholic version back then and who wanted to start each day with a venial sin. Only later did I wonder how my Buddhist friends got through morning prayer but my bet is that by third grade, non-Christian classmates could more or less repeat the *Our Father* and probably had creative ideas about "art in heaven."

I attended weekly Catholic religious classes we called catechism and as I got older, began to notice contradictions in my life. The big one surrounded paisan. Twice a year, Apo bought stacks of colorful squares of tissue paper that we folded into a shape that reminded me of canoes and bananas. Days later when we finished the folding, Apo strung them together and by then, she was busy in the kitchen preparing food to take to the graveyard for KungKung who was buried there.

When we arrived at the Chinese cemetery, she lit joss sticks, laid out the meal she cooked and sprinkled tea and gin around his grave. On his gravestone she placed rice paper with a message in Chinese written by the Taoist priest. While chanting, she burned firecrackers along with the strings of folded papers that represented clothing and money, sending KungKung necessities for the afterlife. She put her hands together, bowed three times and then the rest of us stood in front of his grave one by one, taking turns to bow three times and pay proper respects to our grandfather.

I finally got up the nerve to ask the big question, the one that had been buzzing around my brain: Every week in catechism and at Mass, I would hear that there is only one God and one true church. So how come when Apo arrives with the firecrackers and tissue papers do we go with her to pray for KungKung? That's like going to Chinese church right?

When this question tumbled out, I think the heavens parted with thunderclaps and lightning flashes. My mother the devoted and cradle Catholic stopped what she was doing and turned to give me stink eye and mad mouth. Silent for a long moment, she finally answered, "The reason we go to church AND the graveyard is... to keep peace in the family!"

Abaji, my mother's Korean father didn't attend any church even though Conceição his Portuguese wife raised their seven children as Catholic. But right before he died, he asked to be baptized, not wanting he said, "to be the only one in the family who can't get into Catholic heaven."

A French philosopher once said, "Why not believe... what's to lose?"

Coming from Hilo Hawai`i, I say: Why not believe everything... why take a chance?

CHAPTER 30

SLIPPAHS

I was in Hilo when my teenage son called me from Seattle. "It's an emergency Mom. Somebody took my slippahs last night at the bowling alley."

I wasn't surprised. I could see how everyone would covet those amphibious rubber slippers that we sometimes call zori.

"You know how good they are," my boy continued. "No need socks just jump in and walk out the door."

Of course I knew. I grew up in these slippahs after all. Around Hilo they allow you to walk no sweat over spikey lava rocks into the water then back out on pebbles, sand, through grass and then on top of hot concrete. Zori. Fabulous All-Purpose Footwear.

My son can buy a pair of rubber slippers in Seattle these days for around ten dollars, but in Hilo if I watch for sales, I can pick them up for a buck ninety-nine. He left me with instructions to bring back not just one but two pairs of the exact same black zori size 11, just in case he gets ripped off again. My heart swelled with pride at my son's choice of footwear. But this after all was the boy born in Hilo who spent his first four years in the Islands. His first pair of "shoes" were these slippahs, the baby kind with the strap in the back. In fact, that was all he wore until I bought him a pair of sneakers as soon as we decided to move to Seattle.

As I put on socks then tied the shoes to his feet, I told him, "Better start getting used to these now. Can't wear slippahs in Seattle you know."

I was wrong. You CAN wear rubber slippers in Seattle, sensibly maybe five months out of the year. But sometimes when I drive past one of the colleges in the city popular with students from the Islands, I see them walking around dressed in a ski jacket, scarf, knit cap, thermal gloves, and…shorts with slippahs.

I feel like rolling down my window and yelling, "Ey! It's February and this is Seattle, not Hale`iwa! Put on some shoes and long pants before I call your madah!"

But no sense. They're not going to listen to me.

I smile when I see those island students on campus in the Northwest because I get it about the footwear. Not only are slippers more comfortable than shoes but they make you walk a certain way – the way you walk when you are in the Hawaiian Islands with that loose rhythmic and comforting slap-slapping. So these college students are just being their local best and my warning against wearing slippahs in Seattle in February is merely a practical matter. Your toes could get wet, then freeze, then fall off.

That is something to consider but this is what I know: It's easy to change our shirt but hard to change our shoes.

CHAPTER 31
AUTO NOTE

In Seattle, one of the essential items for the auto is a pen and a small, spiral notebook. You never know when you'll need to write a message to that car taking up two parking spaces. How gratifying to scribble "Who taught you how to park?" on a scrap of paper to leave under the driver's side windshield wiper.

But in Hilo there is no need to carry any pen or paper in your automobile. First of all, the heat will force the ink to ooze out of the ballpoint and permanently puddle between the seats so every time you pull up the handbrake, you'll get an inky mess on your fingers. And I would never leave who-taught-you notes on parked cars because I probably know who taught you how to park. It was some relative of mine.

In Seattle, the only other tool you'll find inside the car other than a pen or pencil is the device to check the pressure in your tires. But in Hilo, every auto I'm in has a spoon or chopstick in the side door pocket even though this is the place where fingers work fine for feeding. There will also be blunt-edge kindergarten scissors for kids (or you) to cut open the cellophane pack of pickled peach you just bought. Pop the trunk and in Seattle, you find the spare tire and all of its trimmings; in Hilo there will also be goza and towels, just in case we get the urge to jump in the ocean on a hot day. In Seattle no one is allowed to eat in my car. In Hilo we're not only eating but sweating and sometimes dripping salt water all the way home.

I can park my car in downtown Hilo for free all day long but if you find no-pay parking in Seattle, you should immediately check body parts to see if perhaps you've transitioned into the Twilight Zone. A few years ago, meter parking rates went up to $1.50 an hour which was bad enough but then the new meters took only quarters! Seattleites scrambled for those sacred coins to hide somewhere under the seat, praying that their teenagers wouldn't poach twelve of them for a three-dollar cup of coffee. That's not counting the six quarters they used to feed the meter so they could lounge in the café, leisurely sipping their double shot espresso truffle mocha.

Seattle has since come to its senses and replaced these ill-conceived parking meters but who can forget those dark days when we were forced to hoard quarters and squirrel them away from loved ones.

On the other hand when I go to downtown Hilo, I can some-times find a free and open parking space right in front of the store where I need to shop. And not so long ago at one of those rare places with metered parking, I used to feed in a penny for enough time to run a fast errand. If I was out of pennies and forced to slip a nickel into the coin slot, that was OK too because I could linger long enough to watch that needle fly, now that I was in no rush. Recently these Hilo meters were also updated so I no longer savor the thrill of flying needles. But with a dime, I can still delight at the sight of minutes running up into double digits. With more than I need, I take my time and stroll around town, checking all the store windows and stopping to talk to friends and shop owners.

But if you see me on the street in downtown Seattle, don't call out because I'll be in a hurry, either scurrying to the store to quickly buy whatever is on my list or hauling shopping bags back to the car. And with one eye always on the parking meter, there is no café loitering for me.

Occasionally I'll notice stretching exercises going on in a car stopped beside me at a traffic light in Seattle: driver twisting his torso first to the left, sometimes locking the door with his right hand when he catches me staring then turning from his waist in the other direction, reaching with wiggling fingers far into the back seat. I can hear bones cracking even over the din of downtown traffic and radio road reports.

But in Hilo, the only car stretching I see is in front of me at the drive-through window, the driver straining to hand over a five-dollar bill, the fast food clerk doing a long reach out with the jumbo shake and fries.

In Seattle, an automobile is stressful; in Hilo, it's fun.

CHAPTER 32

CAT EYE

I was gliding by the fine jewelry case at the Goodwill Store in Seattle when something long-forgotten called out to me. It was a pin from my childhood, a yellow, green and brown cat eye in the center of a cluster of small pink and white shells.

"Uncle Norman" I mumbled, I thought to myself until my thrift-shopping friend said, "Your uncle's here?"

He wasn't but now I had to tell her about Uncle Norman and how he used to bring back shells from Down Under where he worked for six months at a time during the 1950s.

"Your uncle worked in Australia?" my friend asked.

"No, no, no...near Micronesia, the Marshall Islands." I answered, reminding myself about one of my teaching duties: lining up definitions to make sure everybody is working with the same one, although all my cousins in Hilo know where Down Undah is and the Goodwill store is not where I usually worry about definitions. Besides, this was my friend; did I have to check out her definitions too? And the answer apparently is yes because she is one of my Seattle and not Hawai`i friends.

Uncle used to leave Hilo for six months at a time. He flew to O`ahu then was shuttled out to small, isolated islands to the south west where he and other local men were contracted to help the U.S. military build missile and testing sites. We didn't know any details about his job back then because neither did he and all we remember is that Uncle disappeared for a while and then returned with wads of money. We looked forward to his home-coming. Upon arrival he took out a roll of cash, peeled off then handed out to us kids ten and twenty dollar bills, more money than any of us ever had at one time. For the grownups - his wife, sisters, brothers and friends - he brought pearl and jade jewelry along with newfangled electronics: transistor radios and the lat-est cameras. Because there was not much to do on those lonely islands when they were not building, they went diving so Uncle re-turned with giant shells that the aunties proudly displayed in their houses. As for the cat eyes, he said they were scattered all over the beaches, collected and turned into jewelry by guys with time on their hands. Because they look like cat eyes, that's what we called them. It was only much later that I learned that they were not eyes but foot closures created by a sea snail known as the Turban shell.

Memories of Uncle Norman and Down Undah came rushing back to me just because of that one cat eye sitting there in the Goodwill showcase. Naturally I bought it and wear the pin regu-larly since just about everything matches with a yellow, green and brown cat eye nestled in a bed of pink and white, don't you think? And even though one of my Seattle friends called them "shell spit-tle," I still liked them and started searching shops in the Pacific Northwest for these alluring eyes, thanks to the warm memories of Uncle Norman they evoked.

Later at a bookstore in my Seattle neighborhood, the clerk was admiring my pin but after she asked me what it was and I answered, "A cat eye," she became quiet and a little nervous I thought. In fact, she stopped talking and refused to look at me after that. And even though I am a regular customer there, it was for me the end of the workday and I was tired of having to check out other people's definitions. I often ask her to order books with Pacific Island titles and names that I have to spell out so I know she remembers me. But now I'll be the Cat Eye Lady and I bet when she sees me coming, she'll be hiding that fat old orange cat that sleeps in a puddle of sunlight under her window.

Yeah and she bettah because I'm always looking for cat eyes you know, from Down Undah.

CHAPTER 33

NATURAL BEAUTY

I'm sure you won't be surprised to learn that I am not a glamorous person. I used to do some work in radio and all that fame and fortune that comes with being a radio personality... actually I know nothing about it. And frankly, one of the appealing things about being on the airwaves is that for all the listeners know, I could be standing at the microphone in puka pants, no brush teeth, hair all boro boro. It was one of the things I liked about radio work.

But even when I go out in public I don't wear much makeup, a touch of lipstick and that's it. I tell my husband who takes longer to get ready than I do, his ten minutes to my five, that it is because I am a natural beauty. This always causes him endless mirth and merriment. But adding to the beauty – I remind him – I'm also entertainingly amusing (or amusingly entertaining. I still can't decide which one.) At this point he's on the floor on his back, legs kicking upward and arms flailing and I'm never sure if he's enjoying himself immensely or having a convulsion.

I think my aversion to makeup comes from growing up in a place where you can spend an hour painting your face only to have it melt away soon after you step out in 80° heat. And it is pointless to put on mascara when your plan is to jump into the ocean first chance you have. There's nothing glamorous about coming up for air looking like Halloween. I try to find lipstick that is not too jarring so as not to look like the Cheshire cat but then it's gone with my first chug of water. I learned long ago that applying makeup was useless and only worked if I painted up then sat still and did nothing.

So you see why my bathroom counter has very few beauty aids although I confess a fondness for grainy face washes. I found one the other day, something I must have bought a while ago since I was surprised to find it in the cabinet. It was moss colored and smelled of mint and as I washed my face with it, I loved its roughness, good for cleaning out clogged pores. Later when I was driving to work, I kept running my hand over my face, marveling at the softness of my cheeks, my forehead, even my chin. Waow. This was a find and I made a note to take another look when I got home so I could watch for sales.

That evening, I went to my medicine cabinet and pulled out the green tube to read the label and there it was: mint therapy for...feet. FEET. Not FACE, although with both four letter words beginning with F, you can see how I made the mistake. But how did I miss that picture of a footprint?

So here is my dilemma. Can I use a foot scrub on my face? Let me amend this because I know what the beauty experts will say. "Of course not what are you...crazy?! Your feet are the hardest working part of your body and need a good rough scrub but it's too harsh for a face that just sits around all day long doing nothing but talk talk talk!"

Let me instead ask those of you like me, natural beauties who hardly buy these products and hate to waste one already in the cabinet.

Can I?

CHAPTER 34

MANGO

In the middle of a Seattle winter, a student from Mexico brought me a mango and together we admired this perfect, tropical fruit. I turned it this way and that, noting its distinctive shape; she let her fingers caress the smooth green skin that had only the tiniest blush of red and yellow. "In Mexico when it is green like this, we sprinkle it with salt," she said, smacking her lips.

"In Hawai`i, we dip this one in a sauce of shoyu, vinegar and black pepper," I replied, my jaw tightening with the memory. "And if it's a bumper crop year, an auntie will make pickled mango with this green kine."

Another teacher overheard our conversation and stopped in his tracks. "Salt? Vinegar? Pickles? Who does that to a mango?" La Mexicana pursed her lips and I saw in her eyes that my co-worker would never be receiving from her one of nature's delectable perfections. I was glad. Mais fica.

Growing up in Hilo I remember riding with my father down to Lyman Field to pick up the boxes of mangoes sent by his sister in Honolulu. Auntie had a small house on a tiny lot in Pālolo Valley but in her yard were two tall mango trees, one Haden, the other Pirie. During summer visits, I was lulled to sleep in her back bedroom by the sound of falling mango as it rustled through branches of thick leaves then landed with a plop or a splat.

We knew how hard it was to get to these mangoes before they fell. In Auntie's yard was a long bamboo stick with a hook at the tip fashioned from a wire clothes hanger and underneath, a sturdy cloth bag securely tied to the pole. To prevent bruising, the mango picker went after only one mango at a time. The long pole was aimed, hook above the fruit, then one yank and the prize dropped into the bag. If by chance other mangoes fell from the disturbance, whoever was helping with the picking had to run and try to catch them all before they hit the ground. That part was always hilarious.

Auntie sent the delicate fruit to Hilo every summer. The carefully chosen mangoes were wrapped in newspaper, boxed and shipped to family on the outer islands. We picked them up and gently unpacked the boxes when we got home, handling the precious cargo with greater care than the finest crystal. As we sorted them into piles to be shared with friends and relatives, we admired and appraised each, one by one, making sure everybody got some ripe and some green.

While there were mangoes on the Big Island, they were nothing like the Piries and Hadens that arrived each summer from Pālolo Valley. And now that I am older, I understand the trouble it took back then to pick, wrap, pack and ship these fruit from one island to another. Mahalo nui Auntie.

Today, Auntie's trees are gone along with many others around the islands that have been cut down, bowing to demands not only of development and construction but also of manicured lawns not welcoming to overripe fruit. So my student from Mexico gave me not just a mango, but a memory of mango.

Muchas gracias Hija.

CHAPTER 35

THONGS

When my Seattle friend at the college where we work told me she was going to India during monsoon season, I advised her to take along some rubber slippers, just in case. Why ruin those nice walking shoes?

"Oh, do you mean thongs?" She asked.

"Uhmmm…is that what you call them? Yeah, I guess so." I replied. I might think of my favorite footwear as slippahs or zori, but never thongs. Besides, aren't those what we use to turn the shoyu chicken on the barbecue grill?

Later that afternoon when we were done with our classes, I saw her rush past the office window to land one hard knock on my door.

Giggling as she entered, she said, "I asked my students if they know where I can buy some rubber thongs and one of them suggested, 'Victoria's Secret?'"

We had a good laugh at the possibility that students were now wondering what their makule gray-haired teachers were wearing under sensible sweaters and long skirts, imagining us browsing Victoria's Secret racks. (Sales racks of course because we are after all, teachers.) I made a note to not refer to our favorite island footwear as "thongs" until I remembered that never in a million years would I ever call it that. It's a word not even in my vocabulary.

It reminded me of another incident years ago when I was on the student end of these word mix-ups. I had just arrived for my freshman year at the University of Washington and went to the nearest drugstore to buy some feminine necessities. As I paid the cashier, I asked her to please put everything in a package. She looked at me oddly and repeated, "A package?" "Yes" I replied, thinking about the climb back up the hill to get to the dorm. My roommate from east of the Cascade Mountains whom I had just met, pointed to my stuff and said, "You want her to put that in...a package?"

"Yeah," I slowly answered, brain starting to click into action that something was up but without a clue what it might be. And then, drawing from my repository of resourceful critical thinking skills, I thought: Maybe up here in Seattle, they don't use packages and perhaps I should have brought a bigger purse.

My helpful roommate then said, "You want her to gift-wrap your things?"

"No...just put them in a package."

Finally somewhere in the dark, a light went on for my new friend from Yakima. "Oh, you mean a bag! You want her to put your things in a *bag!*"

"Yeah, a package," I repeated, wondering what the big deal was. Stores in Hilo put all the things you purchase in a package.

Semantics. What a hoot. Or is that...a *toot?*

CHAPTER 36

SPIRITS

I was at an old hotel in Kona, admiring the Hawaiian artifacts in the display cases around the lobby. Here were drawings of King Kamehameha, Ka`ahumanu, a fleet of canoes in Kealakekua Bay; there were poi pounders and `umeke sitting on lauhala and rounded stones on kapa for `ulu maika. I was immersed in these reminders of days gone by which is why I like to stop at this hotel perched on the beach near the boat launch. The marlin fishing charters come in nearby and on the other side is a heiau that looks like it is floating right off the shore. But as I was slowly making my way through the lobby going from one exquisite remnant of Hawaiian history to the next, I became aware of a voice barking into the telephone, getting louder as I approached the cases nearby.

"I've had it with this place! Too hot, too humid, too many bugs, too much traffic..." I looked over in the corner at a beefy man red-faced and sweaty, in khaki shorts, a colorful aloha shirt and sandals. He was clearly agitated. I tried not to listen but couldn't help it because I wanted to check out the `ili `ili and `ulī`ulī in the case next to where he was standing and shouting.

He continued, "I'm sick of the food, the people are rude and I just need to get outta here. Good thing Dad got himself on a plane back to the Mainland before he died. I would hate to think about his spirit stuck here, wandering around forever in this crap joint."

This is where my ears perked up. Never mind the sickening food, the rude people, the crap joint, but he was glad his father didn't die here; otherwise, his spirit would be stuck in Kona? I could cut him some slack because perhaps he was still grieving and not thinking clearly but for me, logic and reason were starting to overpower nostalgia. Now I had to stop wallowing in artifacts and pay attention to reality.

I am no expert on spirituality or spirits and in fact, understand that people who are authorities in one might disavow the other. But let's just say I have a fondness for the notion that departed loved ones are following me around, warmly whispering in my ear. Regardless of what you believe however, one thing I thought we would all agree on is that once they're in the spirit world, they don't need no plane ticket coach class if they want to come with me to – say, Seattle. But our irate friend in the black shirt with kalakoa mai tais was worrying that his father's spirit could have been stuck in Kona! Different ideas undoubtedly, about spirits (and shirts.)

The plan is to be on my island when the time comes for me to depart this planet although this won't be happening too soon I hope. And yet, we all know that the best schemes can go awry. But just in case my timing is off, I'm not worried because if somehow I check out in a foreign land, I'll get back here one way or another even if I have to flap my ears and fly.

I wanted to offer condolences and reassure our aggrieved visitor that perhaps his father would not have been forever stuck in Kona even if he had passed on here but maybe this was not the right time and as I moved on to check out the pololū, the lei o manō, I wondered where such ideas come from.

CHAPTER 37

PIN

Here's a question in the headline of a Seattle newspaper fashion column:

WHERE MAY A PIN GO?

Where may a pin go...One of the strategies I teach my students is to try and guess the answer to questions stumping them when they're reading. So, where *may* a pin go? Front? Back? Top? Bottom? Head? Shoulders Knees and Toes, Knees and Toes?

Having now followed my teaching advice of predicting information, I can proceed to reading the answer. Mercifully, it starts off like it could have been written by me. "Feel free to wear pins wherever you choose..." I heave a huge sigh of relief because my answer to *Where may a pin go* is: anywhere you feel like it. But my relief is short-lived. In the next paragraph, the writer recommends coordinating pins with earrings and advises against wearing a pin and a necklace. Too much! Too much!" insists the fashion maven.

Because I'm fascinated by people who think in ways different from mine, I plow on to the next question which asks, "Can my husband wear both suspenders and a belt?" I ponder this from my

Hilo point of view and wonder why would he wear either one? But hey, if your husband wants to wear both, I say double the pleasure and double the fun.

A third question asks where to put a wrist corsage. Even I know the answer to this one. But wait! The fashion-insecure needs clarification. Right or left wrist? Ai Sus!

For all the fashion-fretters reading this story, please earmark this page because I am now going to give my version of answers to these questions and you can pass them on to your friends. My replies are in *italics*.

So. Where may a pin go? *Anyplace you like... shoulder, sleeve, cuff, knees all seem fine.*

How many rings or earrings do you put on? *As many as you want on ears, nose, toes, piko etc.*

Should you wear a belt and suspenders too? *Yes by all means, especially if they hold up your pants. Or no if you like to live dangerously.*

And where do you wear flowers? *Closer to your nose is better than farther. Unless you want to be considerate of others and in that case put them in your armpit.*

If you still have fashion-related questions begging for illumination, please email them to me at ainokea.edu.

CHAPTER 38

SHADE

I like the sun but nothing beats the shade. At least when I'm home in Hawai`i, shade is my preference. When I go to the beach, I always unfurl my goza in a shady spot and prop my cooler against a tree trunk where there is shade. When I'm looking for a parking space, I take the shady one even if it's farther away. I try to avoid the first degree burns that can result when my hands grab hold of a steering wheel that's been broiling in the blazing sun. If the only space is out in the open, I get the beach towel from the trunk and drape it over the wheel in order to avoid driving home later by steering with only one fingertip. I hate it when hard candy sitting in the hot sun melts on car seats or in side pockets because then you'll sit on sticky sugar and find it coating those pennies and nickels you're saving for the occasional parking meter. I like to hang my clothes out on a line to dry but am careful to put my favorite colored pieces in the shade. I usually wear a hat when I'm outside and put a shirt over my swimsuit when I'm not in the water. "Kapu the shade!" is what I hear when kids are running to find their lunch spot.

I'm always surprised when I see at parades and other outdoor events in the Islands those who seek the sun. These are usually folks without enough melanin who should in fact be in the shade. But even when there's room under my tree, I notice the ones who unfold their webbed chairs far away from it way out in the middle of an open grassy area, relentless sun forcing beads of sweat to dot their nose and forehead. Or I see them staking out territory on the hard, unforgiving but sunny concrete that conducts the heat waves right back through their feet up to the head so that even their hair looks hot.

At the beach, I worry about people frying in oil. I see them turn bright red and sometimes burn to a crisp. I hear them siz-zling as I walk by. They look like they're sleeping out there on the sand and I wonder how they'll be sleeping tonight. I want to yell SHADE! SHADE! But they'll only think I'm trying to steal their spot.

I understand where some of this comes from because when I'm in Seattle, I like the sun too, especially since we can go days with-out seeing it. The shade up there is often cold and when I sit in it even on a warm day, I might need a sweater. This is probably why a sunny day gets so much attention in the Pacific Northwest. *Isn't this weather great?* is a common greeting on those rare days. And don't tell the boss but I even hear *Maybe I should call in sick so I can catch some rays.* I am aware that sunshine is one way to get essential vitamin D. It's not the only way but I will concede that it's more pleasant than broccoli.

Around Puget Sound, everybody talks about the sun, but no-body mentions the shade. In Hawai`i, we talk about neither and yet what most of us know, is while sun is good, shade is even better. But have you ever heard anyone say, "Hey, let's go soak up some shade!"

Maybe I'll start a new trend.

Or maybe I'll just keep quiet and open up my beach chair in the cool, luscious shade under that wide and glorious banyan tree.

CHAPTER 39

BIG SLEEP

I have to report that the traffic is getting bad, even in Hilo. I'm surprised because in Seattle no matter how often people honked, glared or sent finger messages, I always knew that I could come home to Hilo for some relaxing cruising around town. And while it is still possible to do so, I now occasionally find myself stuck in traffic on the wet side of the Big Island and here is what I've noticed: Car owners in Hilo are sometimes using their automobile as a memorial to loved ones. As I wait behind or beside another car in my home town, I often read on the back window or the side door, a message for a dearly departed. *In Loving Memory Of...* then a name, followed by the date of birth and death and then something like: *Forever in our hearts* or *We will always love you.*

In case you think this is new, don't be fooled; it is only a new form of something old. In Hilo, I drive around in my mother's car with my father's jacket always in the back seat. Dad died a few years ago but Mom leaves his jacket in the car "so he can come with us when we go holoholo," she says. And not only does he keep us company but he continues to take care of us. As we're out and about, she and I have on separate occasions put Dad's jacket on in an unexpected chilly rain shower. But this new-style memorial painted on the back windows and sides of cars and trucks is fairly recent and it makes me smile. This is my hometown of Hilo Hanakahi where we do things a little differently. It is only one of the reasons why I love it.

If you drive around the Big Island, you will notice shrines alongside the road, sometimes a cross with a lei draped over it, sometimes a toy motorcycle next to a bouquet of flowers or balloons. Down at the beach, there are coconut trees with a small hand-printed plaque nailed to them and same as on the cars: name, date of birth and death, a loving message. And always, flowers nearby. If you cruise past in the early evening, you might see locals gathering to talk story and share a beer after work with their absent friend now missing and missed, who left them too early at that very spot.

In Seattle, I might see an occasional outdoor shrine but there aren't other memorial signs by the side of the highway that I've ever observed. And if there are, we're driving too fast to notice. But even when I'm stuck in traffic, there are no written messages about loved ones on the cars in front of or next to me. All I might see on one of the doors or windows are business ads and phone numbers for Big Blossoms or Dandy Desserts. The painted memorials on cars and the roadside gathering of friends are only in the Islands and I'm glad to see these heartfelt reminders of those who have moved on.

Some people don't like this. Distractions, they say and why not just take your memories and flowers to the cemetery like everybody else. Cemetery – a word from Greek and Latin meaning "the sleeping place." Some of us in Hilo still call it the graveyard. Not as poetic but perhaps more accurate.

I'm happy to see roadside shrines and memorials on automobiles in Hawai`i. I am always *in* a car when I see these and it reminds me that the Big Sleep could be right around the corner. Better slow down.

CHAPTER 40

COFFEE

Call me prejudiced but for the best coffee beans in the world, head over to the Island of Hawai`i where coffee trees grow in cracks between lava rocks up mauka, at the edge of the rain forest on the slopes of Hualālai. Call me biased but Kona is where the best beans come from. And recently near Ka Lae on the southern part of the island, Ka`ū farmers have started producing coffee rising in prominence so Hawai`i islanders now have our pick of prize-winning beans. There are even a few farms in Hilo and along the Hāmākua coast so if you love the whole coffee-growing culture, then lucky you live Hawai`i!

However, if you feel the urge to *drink* coffee, then make your way to the Capital of Coffee Consumption, to Seattle, Washington. This is the place where the coffee hits the cup and the cup and the cup and the cup. Seattleites don't need ID cards to prove that they live there. They just whip out their frequent coffee card where paying for twelve cups gets them the thirteenth free.

Anywhere else I order coffee like this: a cup of coffee please. But if I order it that way in Seattle, I might as well wear a sign around my neck that says Just Visiting. Instead, I must say something like "a triple shot espresso" or "a tall macchiato with soy." Seattleites drink so much coffee that forget New York, *Seattle* should be The City that Never Sleeps. And not content with getting a fix from the rich dark brew, coffee lovers also indulge in that ultimate rush, chocolate-covered coffee beans. One bite and your eyes snap open and your mouth springs into action, even during the most boring of meetings where you don't care about the topic and previously had nothing to say about it.

On the other hand, in Hilo I just have coffee, mostly in the mornings. And in a place where world-famous coffee beans are grown, you would think that Big Islanders have as large a coffee vocabulary as do people in Seattle, but we don't. When I go to one of the outlets on the Kona coast, I might throw around words like *100%, whole bean, medium roast, peaberry,* but that's nothing compared to how I coffee talk in Seattle. There I know the difference between *latte* and *cappuccino, americano* and *italiano.* I show off my fancy lexicon with *barista, biscotti, solo, doppio.* But if I use words like these on the Big Island, I might as well be speaking Italian.

For all you coffee lovers out there, let me offer you an opportunity for the supreme java experience. Come to Hawai`i Island for a week to *pick* coffee. Forget the snorkeling and sunning on the beach. Don't bother with resort clothes. Pack instead your oldest most comfortable puka shoes and clothing and head up mauka where the coffee land is. Spend all your daylight hours in the broiling sun, balancing on loose lava rocks and carefully pulling down the loaded coffee branch with the guava stick to lovingly pick by hand each cherry one by one while clearing away spider webs and shooing off bees. I guarantee you a memorable experience, more riveting than watching whales, more mystical than viewing volcanoes, more aerobic than hiking Mauna Loa.

Want to appreciate coffee? That's how.

CHAPTER 41

OCEAN

I can't be far away from the ocean. I found this out the hard way by agreeing once to live in Colorado. When I told neighbors how I missed the water, they directed me to a nearby lake where everyone goes for their summer swimming. But when I arrived there, I found it crowded with families floating their towels on the tall grasses which fringed the lake and children gleefully jumping into the brown and murky water where I was sure frogs and other amphibians were lurking.

"C'mon! Let's go in!" invited my well-meaning neighbor.

"Ummmm...maybe I'll pass," was my weak response. "I'm not used to such ice cold water." Which was bull lie because Hilo has a popular swimming spot freezing cold from spring water called Ice Pond but I didn't tell her.

Every vacation from Colorado included the long drive over mountains and through deserts out to the West Coast. My family eventually figured out that I needed to be near not just any ocean but the wide and wonderful Ka Pākipika and finally, we went back to Hawai`i.

But then came the opportunity to move to Seattle which I thought was safe since Washington State is on the Pacific Ocean and from our house we could walk to Puget Sound which technically is not quite but almost this same body of water.

While we were still unpacking, I decided to take the children to the nearest beach on our first hot day of summer. They cheered as I loaded up the car with towels, sunscreen, goza, a cooler of juice, a box with musubi and chicken, just like in Hawai`i. The car had hardly come to a rolling stop at Golden Gardens when the kids spilled out and ran down to the beach. The youngest who was four and had known only warm Hawaiian waters, splashed in but then just as quickly splashed back out. Storming up to me, he put his icy hands on my face.

"You call this a beach?" he accused, blue lips trembling, eyes welling up with tears. The older two stayed a little longer, about another minute, then came out, wrapped themselves tightly in their towels and hopped around to warm up. Even the musubi and chicken tasted different.

I told my kids that at least the ocean is the same. May*be,* they conceded, but going to the beach is not.

Auwē.

CHAPTER 42

MARIGOLD

My mother sent me a photo of herself proudly posing next to her patch of marigolds in Kaūmana. She worked hard to get a few small plants to take root and bloom among the lava rocks in her backyard. I dared not tell her that in Seattle, I am not so thrilled with these golden sprigs and am never quite sure who snuck them into my front lawn. I know they repel garden pests and can even be edible and yes they fend off deer and other animals, but door-to-door fundraisers for obscure causes still make their way to my house, following a path brightly lit I am sure by those glaring neon clusters.

Later when I flew in from Washington, I dutifully complimented her horticultural achievement then asked about the spray of velvet lavender catteleyas perched on the rock wall way in the back of the lot. "Tell you the truth I didn't even know those orchids were there with all the huapala and laua`e," she said, glancing in their direction before bending to pull some weeds that were threatening her precious marigolds.

I suppose it's harder to grow marigolds in Hilo than orchids that bloom willy-nilly. But that is how these show-offs are. Just leave them alone and they'll thrive which is why Hawai`i Island is known as the Orchid Isle. A few years ago my father decided he couldn't keep up with the maintenance of the bottle brush trees around the yard, having to trim and constantly rake, so I helped him cut and haul them to the dump. Because there were a few orchid plants clinging to their base, we didn't cut the trees down completely but instead, left the trunks about three feet high. Without us doing anything more than that, the orchids have steadily crept up and around the stumps. This year I noticed the trunks are now completely covered with orchid plants and my mother says that when they bloom, people stop to admire.

In Seattle I have two potted orchids, given to me by well-meaning friends to counter my regular bouts of Hawai`i homesickness. I would have never bought them for myself because of the care and attention those plants need in the Pacific Northwest. First I have to water them but not too much. Sit them in a damp, rocky bed in indirect northern sunlight; feed them just the right amount of orchid food at the right time; water spray regularly to fool them into thinking it is the humid air they like to breathe. Some people even talk and sing to them (but not me.)

Up there, orchids have the reputation of being delicate, temperamental, sultry beauties requiring special care. And expensive! A pot with a single spray can cost fifty bucks so you bet I pay attention to those two gifts given with good intentions.

I can choose an orchid plant from a dozen varieties and pick it up for three dollars at the Hilo Farmers' Market. On one visit, I couldn't resist a green cymbidium and brought it up to Kaūmana for my mother to enjoy. But on my next trip in when I asked about it, she confessed that she threw it by the back wall where the lavender catteleya was blooming. I realized this was her dumping ground for all the plants I brought home whenever I visited! But no matter because in Hilo we can ignore the orchids and they are still going to burst out regularly in a riot of shapes and colors.

But the marigolds? *These* we have to pay attention to. You would think by the way my mother babies them that they were rare and exotic.

I guess to her, they are.

CHAPTER 43

YOUTH

The French have let me down. How could they, after I went so far as to learn the subjunctive of être and avoir? I just read somewhere that EVEN THE FRENCH! who used to believe that aging was a good thing – in cheese and wine for example – have now joined the Hollywood-crazed populations putting a premium on youth.

Not fair because when I was growing up in Hilo, I was completely unaware that being young was an advantage. In fact, I used to think that youth was like Waikīkī – a place that everyone has to pass through once but you don't want to stay too long.

I remember mouthing off an opinion when I was a teenager and told that I was too young to know what I was talking about. Then there was the time some Korean musicians came through Hilo and I learned that one of them had already been declared "Intangible Cultural Treasure" in Korea, but could not officially assume the mantle until she turned fifty. No wonder I looked forward to growing older.

But now that I've passed the age where I could be Intangible Cultural Treasure, it seems that everyone else is searching for their lost youth. While my youth may be gone, it is not lost; I left it behind on purpose. And yet, with the baby boomers turning 60, all I'm hearing and reading about are ways not only to stop the clock but even to turn it back. Back to when I was forced to do long division, diagram sentences, practice musical scales and read books with titles like "The Mill on the Floss"? Back to a time I couldn't walk anywhere without a little person hanging onto my leg? When food hunting, gathering and preparing occupied most of my waking hours? Don't get me wrong. That was all good fun and I was glad to be doing it then. But now, I'm happy to be here in my senior moment facing forward thank you.

A few years ago, Elsie's Fountain on Mamo Street in Hilo was sold by its long-time owners, an elderly couple who had been running the place for as long as I can remember. Before it changed hands, I would stop by for some comfort food and warm memories because nothing much was different from the 1960s – not the red Formica and chrome counter with matching swivel stools, not the faded food pictures on the wall, not the green milk shake and malted mixer. I would say that the only new thing they added before finally packing up was a sign propped on a chair by the door, hand-printed on brown cardboard that read:

Life begins at 80.

I think they're on to something.

CHAPTER 44

HA`INA

I enjoy music, but that's no surprise. Have you ever met anyone from Hawai`i who didn't? While I was growing up in Hilo, it seemed as though my days and nights were filled with music. Like a lot of families, we had an old piano in the living room that everybody plinked on. Waiākeawaena, one of Hilo's elementary schools, had `ukulele lessons built into the curriculum so all the students there learned to play that beloved Portuguese-Hawaiian instrument. At Hilo Intermediate School, everyone had to sign up for chorus or band so the neighborhoods were filled with sounds of students singing or practicing the trombone, clarinet, tuba. Wherever we were – home, school, beach, park, stairway, sidewalk – music filled the air.

Later when I went off to college, I tried to expand my musical horizons by going to the opera but I couldn't get past the story. "Just enjoy the music!" exasperated friends would say but I was constantly distracted by details. "OK those cherry blossoms look nice but that woman in the kimono is stepping too wide and her boobs are too big." And the story didn't make any sense. I kept suppressing the urge to shout, "Don't do it Butterfly!"

And then there was the symphony where the music was heavenly but I could never be sure exactly when it ended. Is it done... do I clap now? Oh no, not yet... they're starting up again. Wait wait wait...is that clapping I hear? I think I can clap...is it OK... can I clap now?

It was like a trick exam question that I kept flunking.

This never happens with Hawaiian music because of ha`ina. Whether we are singing, dancing or just listening, when we hear ha`ina, we know it is the last verse because almost all Hawaiian songs end with ha`ina. It simply means: *this is the end of my song* or *now my story is over.* Sometimes you will hear ha`ina hou where the final verse is repeated, just so you know to make no mistake about it. That's it, pau this song.

So this is my ha`ina, my last story. And perhaps at an intersection on the island you will run into a makule with Hilo stamped on her forehead and that could be me, looking right and left, up and down, this way and that. You might think I am wondering which way to go but no. I'm just catching the breeze, waving to a friend, admiring the mountain, watching the ocean because in the end, no question about it, it will always be the Hawai`i way for me.

Aloha, a hui hou.

GLOSSARY

*B*elow is a glossary of local words and definitions used in Hawai`i Ways. Some Hawaiian words have diacritics which affect pronunciation and meaning such as `okina (`) before a vowel that signifies a glottal stop, and kahakō (macron) over a vowel for lengthening. The following letters identify word origins:

H – Hawaiian
P – Pidgin aka Hawaii Creole English
C – Chinese
Po – Portuguese
J – Japanese
K – Korean
F – Filipino

If an unfamiliar capitalized word is not listed here, it is a Hawaiian person or place name.

A

Abaji (K) - father
a hui hou (H) - until the next time
ai Sus (F) – expression of exasperation

ainokea (P) – I don't care
ali`i (H) – chief/royalty
aloha (H) – hello, goodbye, love
Apo (C) - grandmother
auwē (H) – expression of emphasis or sorrow
azuki (J) – red beans

B

bagoong (F) – fermented shrimp sauce
bettah (P) - better
bon dance (J) – dance at Obon festival to honor ancestors
boro boro (J) - messy
brudda/braddah (P) – brother, friend
bumbye (P) – by and by, later

C

char siu (C) – red roast pork
crack seed (P) – dried fruit marinated in Chinese spices
cuz (P) – 1) cousin, friend
    2) because

D

da (P) - the
da kine (P) – context-based; whatever we're talking about
da pepa (P) – the newspaper

F

fadah (P) - father
fo'real (P) – truly, really

G

ganfannit (P) – gosh darn it (or something like that)
goza (J) – straw mat

H

Haina (H) – area makai of Honoka`a
ha`ina (H) – the end of the story/song
ha`ina hou (H) – the end again
haku lei (H) – braided lei
hanabata (J) – nose snot
hanabata (P) - childhood
haole (H) – Caucasian, nowadays white American
hapa (haole) (H) – half white
harm ha (C) - fermented fish sauce
Hawai`i Pono`ī (H) – national anthem of the Hawaiian kingdom
    and state
heiau (H) – sacred temple
holoholo (H) – to go around for fun, pleasure
hongwanji (J) – Buddhist temple
huapala (H) – orange trumpet vine
humuhumunukunukuāpua`a (H) – triggerfish; Hawaii State fish

I

`ili `ili (H) – pebbles used as hula implement

K

kakimochi (J) – rice crackers
kalakoa (H from English calico) – colorful
kalo (H) – taro

kāne (H) - male
kapa/tapa (H) – cloth made from tree bark
Ka Pākīpika (H from English) – the Pacific Ocean
kapu (H) - taboo
kīhō`alu (H) – slack key musical style
kim chee (K) – fermented cabbage
kine (P) – kind, thing
KungKung (C) – grandfather

L

laua`e (H) – a kind of fern
lauhala (H) – leaf of the hala (pandanus) tree, dried and woven
    into mats, fans etc.
laulau (H) – pork and fish wrapped in taro and ti leaf then
    steamed
lei (H) – garland of flowers
lei o manō (H) – weapon of shark's tooth
li hing mui (C) – salted seed
liliko`i (H) – passion fruit
lo`i (H) – irrigated taro field

M

madah (P) - mother
mahalo (H) – thank you
maha`oi (H) – rude; nervy
Mainlin (P) (Mainland) – continental U.S.
makai (H) – toward the ocean
makule (H) – old (person)
malassada (Po) – fried doughnut
manini (H) – small, stingy
mais fica (Po) – more for me

mauka (H) – toward the mountain
musubi (J) – rice ball
mu`u mu`u (H) – loose gown/dress

N

niele (H) – frivolous questioning
nori (J) – dried seaweed
nui (H) - big

O

`ōkole (H) – buttock area
`ōlelo (H) – (Hawaiian) language
omiyage (J) – hostess gift
`ono (H) - delicious
onolicious (P) - delicious
`opihi (H) - limpet
`ōpū (H) - belly
`ōpelu eye (P) – look of suspicion

P

paisan (C) – graveyard ceremony honoring ancestors
palaka (H from English) - plaid fabric used for paniolo shirts
paniolo (H from Spanish, Español) – cowboy
pau (H) – done, finished
piko (H) – belly button
poi (H) – starch staple made from kalo
pololū (H) – long spear
pōmaika`i (H) – good luck
puka (H) - hole
pupule (H) – crazy

S

shaka (P) – friendly hand greeting/signal among locals
shave ice (P) – island snack with ice and fruit syrups, from Japan
sistah/sista (P) – sister/friend
slippah (P) – slipper, usually zori
stink eye (P) – mad look

T

tadaksh (Po) – trinkets
teacha (P) - teacher
tita (P) – local female you don't mess with
Tūtū (H) - grandparent

U

`ukulele (H) – popular string instrument from Azores/Madeira
    adopted by Hawaiians
`ulī `ulī (H) – hula implement with gourd and feathers
`ulu maika (H) – round rock used in maika game
`umeke (H) – wooden bowl, calabash

W

wahine (H) – woman
watchutink (P) – what do you think?
wen (P) – past tense marker

Z

zori (J) – rubber slippers; flip-flops

Made in the USA
Monee, IL
16 February 2020